Richard Jefferies, Grace Toplis

Jefferies' land

A history of Swindon and its environs

Richard Jefferies, Grace Toplis

Jefferies' land
A history of Swindon and its environs

ISBN/EAN: 9783337203566

Printed in Europe, USA, Canada, Australia, Japan

Cover: Foto ©Andreas Hilbeck / pixelio.de

More available books at **www.hansebooks.com**

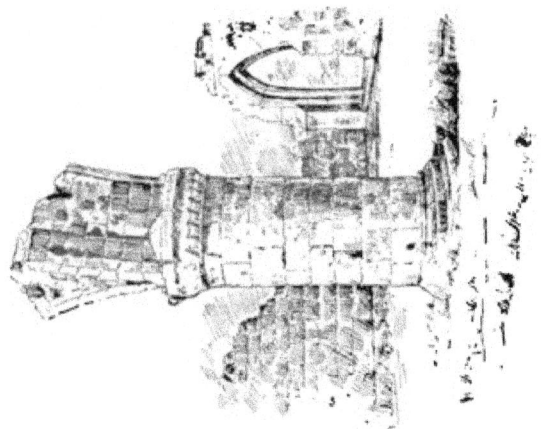

NORMAN PIER,
IVY-CHURCH PRIORY.

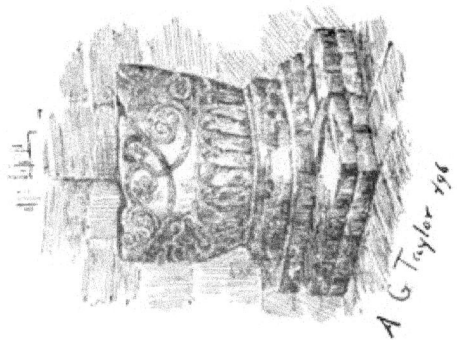

THE FONT,
AVEBURY CHURCH.

A G Taylor '96

JEFFERIES' LAND

A History of Swindon and its Environs

BY THE LATE

RICHARD JEFFERIES

EDITED WITH NOTES BY

GRACE TOPLIS

WITH MAP AND ILLUSTRATIONS

LONDON

Simpkin, Marshall, Hamilton, Kent & Co Ltd

WELLS, SOMERSET: ARTHUR YOUNG

MDCCCXCVI

CONTENTS

LIST OF ILLUSTRATIONS

Note.—The illustrations are reproductions from drawings by Miss Agnes Taylor, Ilminster, mostly from photographs taken especially by Mr. Chas. Andrew, Swindon.

INTRODUCTION

L IFE *teaches no harder lesson to any man than the bitter truth—as true as bitter—that* "A prophet is not without honour, save in his own country, and in his own house." *And foremost among modern prophets who have had to realize its bitterness stands Richard Jefferies, the "prophet" of "field and hedge-row" and all the simple daily beauty which lies about us on every hand. The title of "The Painter of the Downs" might be given to him, as it was to the veteran artist H. G. Hine, for his glorification of his native country in word-pictures as vivid and glowing as the colours on the canvas.*

But Wiltshire never realized, during his lifetime, the greatness of the man whom she had reared, and it is open to question whether she honours his memory now. "I can't see what people find to admire in his books, I can see nothing in them," has been said again and again by those who live among the sights and scenes which he loved so well, and made familiar to jaded readers in the town.

For Sir Walter Besant was right. It is the Londoner who appreciates what Jefferies has to tell of "the Life of the Fields." "Why, we must have been blind all our lives; here were the most wonderful things possible going on under our very noses, but we saw them not. Nay, after reading all the books and all the papers—every one—that Jefferies wrote between the years 1876 and 1887, after learning from him all that he had to teach, I cannot yet see these things. I see a hedge; I see wild rose, honeysuckle, black briony—herbe aux femmes battues, the French poetically call it—blackberry, hawthorn, and elder. I see on the banks sweet wildflowers, whose names I learn from year to year, and straightway forget because they grow not in the streets. I know very well, because Jefferies has told me so much, what I should be able to see in the hedge and on the bank besides these simple things; but yet I cannot see them, for all his teaching. Mine—alas!—are eyes which have looked into shop *windows and across crowded streets for half a century, save for certain intervals every year; they are helpless eyes when they are turned from men and women to flowers, ferns, weeds, and grasses; they are, in fact, like unto the eyes of those men with whom I mostly consort. None of us—poor street-struck creatures—can see the things we ought to see."*

These are the readers who appreciate Jefferies. And of these are formed the elect forty thousand who feel the charm of his written words. "His own country" may question his right to be numbered among her great men, but he is safe in his own niche in the Campo Santo of English Literature, and neither neglect nor disparagement avail now for hurt or wounding. In a handy little Tourist's Guide to Wiltshire, *Mr. R. N. Worth says: "Wiltshire needs not to be ashamed of its worthies," and gives a list of honoured names; but the name of Richard Jefferies is not on his list. "*SAVE *in his own country, and in his own house."*

The spell of Jefferies' Land must be sought in his later books: Wild Life in a Southern County, Wood Magic, Round About a Great Estate, *etc., etc.; or, better still, it may be sought—and found—on a summer's day by any wayfarer on the Downs who possesses a seeing heart and eye.   But, in his early days, Jefferies could find no utterance for the vision which came to him, and yet, even then, in his crudest and most unformed period, he was loyal to his country, and desired to do it honour.   His* History of Swindon and its Environs *was written in the days when he worked for the* North Wilts Herald, *in which the last pages appeared in June,* 1867, *when he had but a boy's second-hand acquaintance with the facts and traditions he collected so laboriously.   "I visit every place I have to refer to, copy inscriptions, listen to legends, examine antiquities, measure this, estimate that; and a thousand other employments essential to a correct account take up my time. . . .   To give an instance.   There is a book published some twenty years ago founded on a local legend.   This I wanted, and have actually been to ten different houses in search of it; that is, have had a good fifty miles' walk, and as yet all in vain.   However, I think I am on the right scent now, and believe I shall get it."*

There was no sparing of time and labour

in this early work of his. Let this be remembered before it receives harsh judgment.

In the preface to The Early Fiction of
Richard Jefferies, *obvious criticism is anticipated, and reasons are given for the republi-
cation of his boyish writings. The latter may
be quoted in this volume.*

" *Why then do these early efforts make their
appearance in this permanent book-form ?*

" *For two reasons; the least worthy of which
is, that a book-lover yearns to make his collection complete, and the Juvenilia of other great
writers are 'taken as read' and placed with
their fellows lest one link should be missing.
But the reason for the student is that they
illustrate—as can be done by no comment from
outsiders—the mental growth of the man, and
his unusually slow development as a writer.
This is why they possess interest in the eyes of
a Jefferiesian student, and why they are offered
to the reading public as* intellectual curios."

The task, therefore, of editing his History
of Swindon *presented some unusual difficul-
ties, due to two facts—that it was written
during the period of his immaturity; and that
thirty years have elapsed since he wrote it.*

The first difficulty lay in the style of his writing, in his authoritative pronouncements on matters antiquarian far beyond the bounds of his boyish knowledge of the past; the second difficulty lay in the changes which thirty years have brought to Swindon, and in the difference between the Then and the Now.

After much consideration, it seemed better to issue the book as his *work, and as he wrote it, with all its merits or faults as the reader may pronounce. To bring the* History of Swindon *up to date, to eliminate all the "facts" which time has disproved, to revise his "antiquarian" statements with the fuller knowledge of a later day, would possibly have resulted in a more useful book of reference, but it would not have been the work of Richard Jefferies. The Editor's task has been confined, therefore, to mere annotation and explanation of what the young Jefferies wrote; and if local antiquarian societies will do it the honour of rectifying crude judgments, and disproved "facts," so much the better for the wider public of readers whom this volume will never reach.*

GRACE TOPLIS.

BIBLIOGRAPHY

In addition to the usual historical works of reference, the following authorities have been consulted :—

Wiltshire, extracted from Domesday Book . . . . . *H. P. Wyndham.*

Wiltshire. The Topographical Collections of John Aubrey, F.R.S. A.D. 1659–70. Corrected and enlarged by J. E. Jackson. 1862 *Aubrey. Jackson.*

Beauties of Wiltshire. 1825 . . *J. Britton.*

The Natural History of Wiltshire. Edited and Elucidated by J. Britton. 1847 . . . . *Aubrey. Britton.*

Tracts relating to Wiltshire. 1856-72. *J. E. Jackson.*

Annales of England. 1615 . . *Stow—Howes.*

History of England under the Norman Kings. Translated from German of Dr. Lappenberg, by Benjamin Thorpe. 1857 . . *Lappenberg. Thorpe.*

Dictionary of National Biography . Ed. *Leslie Stephen.*

Autobiography of John Britton. 1850. *Britton.*

Ancient Hills. Roman Era . . *Sir R. Hoare.*

History of the Rebellion. Edited by Macray. 1888 . . . . *Clarendon.*

History and Antiquities of the Duchy
    of Lancaster. 1817 .   .   .   *Gregson.*

Wiltshire Archæological Magazine:
    "The White Horses of Wiltshire."   *W. C. Plenderleath.*

Reliques of Ancient English Poetry.   *Thomas Percy.*

Six Old English Chronicles. (Ethel-
    werd, Richard of Cirencester,
    etc.) .   .   .   .   .   .   *J. A. Giles.*

The Fairford Windows. Monograph.   *Rev. J. G. Joyce.*

Round the Works of our Great Rail-
    ways .   .   .   .   .   .

Swindon : Fifty Years Ago, More or
    Less .   .   .   .   .   .   *W. Morris,*
                                              Swindon.

HOUSE IN VICTORIA STREET, SWINDON,
where Jefferies lived after his marriage.

JEFFERIES' LAND

CHAPTER I

ANCIENT SWINDON

THE early history of Swindon is involved in obscurity. The works by whose aid the mist of antiquity has in many places been considerably cleared away, until the outline at least, if not the details, of the structure our forefathers reared, is perceivable, here give no assistance. There does not appear to have ever been a monastery at Swindon. Its streets no doubt have been perambulated by the mass-thanes, the hooded noblemen of the cloisters, but they do not seem to have ever taken up a permanent residence.

There is no chronicle of Swindon, so the want which the monks supplied in other places is severely felt here. It is impossible to com-

B

pile an uninterrupted narrative. Facts there
are, and traditions there are, scattered up and
down a long vista of years; but no art, short
of fiction, could combine them into a chronicle.
It does not appear that any great event of
national importance ever took place at Swindon
—no royal murder or marriage; no battle
seems to have been fought, no castle built, not
even a castrament remains in Swindon itself to
bear a witness to bygone deeds of blood—
blood which writes itself so indestructibly
wherever it has been spilt. Hence no writer,
no historian, mentions Swindon, nor gives any
account of it as a place the memory of which
was worth preserving for what had occurred
there.

Even the etymology of the name Swindon
is uncertain. The most probable conjecture
assigns its origin to the Danes. In the year
993 the celebrated Sweyn,[1] king of Denmark,

[1] Swend was the son of Harold Blaatand, and received
at baptism the name of Otto, but he soon cast away the
Christian faith, and waged war on behalf of Thor and Odin.
He probably took a part as a private Viking in the first
three years of piracy which devasted Wessex. Died at
Gainsborough, 1014.
During one of his seasons of adversity he was won back

accompanied by Olave,[1] king of Norway, made his first piratical descent upon the coast of England. Though bought off several times, he invariably returned with increased forces, and at length, coming to Bath, received the homage of the western thanes, or noblemen, and ascended the throne of England. This was in the year 1013 A.D. Sweyn was much of his time in the western counties, hence it is conjectured that Swindon means no more than Sweyn's-don, dune, or hill—the hill of Sweyn. Dune, now usually pronounced don, was a Saxon word for hill—it survives still in *down*, of which there is a sufficiency in the neigh-

to the faith from which he had apostatized, and became a zealous founder of Churches.

Danish writers testify to his piety, but German and English writers are silent on the subject.

For St. Edmund he had a special hatred. In marching to Bury to plunder the minster dedicated to him, he was suddenly stricken with the malady from which he died. Tradition says he had a vision of the saint riding armed to destroy him. His body was embalmed by an English lady, and taken, at her own cost, to Denmark, where it was buried in his own church of Roeskild.

Freeman says of Swend that he was a great man, if greatness consist in mere skill and steadfastness in carrying out an object; his glory is that of an Attila, or a Buonaparte.

[1] Olaf Tryggwasson.

bourhood. Should this conjecture be correct, it would follow that Sweyn must have had some connection with this place, resided here, or made it the scene of some of his exploits. Strange to say, this Sweyn seems to be the first and the last royal celebrity who came into connection with Swindon. In eight centuries nothing of national importance is recorded as taking place here, except this visit of Sweyn, and even that is a matter of supposition. This is tolerably good evidence that the town was for many hundred years of little or no importance. A history of Swindon, properly so-called, would not extend over a period of more than one hundred years : yet the place seems to have existed for eight hundred years. The only way in which its existence can be rendered evident is by tracing the descent of the surrounding landed property from owner to owner.

The first of whom any record appears to exist as possessing land at Swindon was Earl William, a celebrated nobleman in the days of Edward the Confessor, whose reign extended from 1042 to 1066. The domain of Swindon had in all probability previously belonged to the Crown, since it is mentioned that Earl William held it by right of charter, and to the Crown it again returned about 1050 A.D., that nobleman exchanging it for an estate in the Isle of Wight. In what manner it became sub-divided does not seem recorded, but when Domesday Book was compiled by order of William the Conqueror—between 1082 and 1086—the lands at Swindon were in the possession of five persons. Three of these were small, and the remaining two extensive proprietors. All were public men, attendants upon the Conqueror, probably Normans, who came into possession by right of conquest, as a reward for following their master. The first in point of grandeur, celebrity, and the extent of his possessions, was no less a person than Odin,[1] chamberlain to the Conqueror. The

---

[1] Swindon, as referred to in Domesday Book. "Odinus, the chamberlain, holds Svindone. Torbertus held it, T. R. E., and it was affeffed at 12 hides. Here are 6 ploughlands. Two of them are in demefne with 2 fervants. And 6 villagers and 8 borderers occupy 3 ploughlands. The mill pays 4 fhillings. Here are 30 acres of meadow, and 20 acres of pafture. It was valued at 60 fhillings; now at 100. Milo holds 2 hides of this manor, and he has 1 ploughland. Odinus claims them."

[Odinus Camerarius tenet Svindone. Torbertus tenuit

second was the Bishop of Bayeux. Odo,
Bishop of Bayeux—of course a Norman, for at
that date there does not seem to have been a
single British bishop who rendered himself
infamous by his tyranny and ambition. When
an insurrection broke out in the north, occa-
sioned by the intolerable oppression of another
Norman bishop, he of Bayeux marched there
with an army, slaughtered the inhabitants, and
though an ecclesiastic, actually plundered the
cathedral of Durham. He was now found to
have a design on the Papacy, and set sail for
Rome, attended by a retinue of knights and
barons, when King William, who scarcely desired to see a vassal of his an infallible pope,
met him off the Isle of Wight, and seized him
with his own hands.

The bishop cried out that he was a "clerk
and minister of the Lord."

"I condemn not a clerk or a priest, but my
count, whom I set over my kingdom," replied

T. R. E. et geldabat pro 12 hidis. Terra eſt 6 carucatæ.
In dominio ſunt 2 carucatæ, et 2 ſervi. Et 6 villani et 8
bordarii cum 3 carucatis. Ibi molinus reddit 4 ſolidos.
Et 30 acræ prati, et 20 acræ paſturæ. Valuit 60 ſolidi;
modo 100. De hac terra tenet Milo 2 hidas et ibi habet
1 carucatam. Odinus eas calumniatur.]

the king, and he was sent as a prisoner to Normandy.[1]

[1] Stow, in his *Annales of England*, says :—" About this time many tempests raging in the world, certaine Sooth-saiers of Rome declared who should succeed unto Hilde-brand in the Popedom, they affirmed after the decease of Gregorie, Odo to bee Pope of Rome. Odo Bishoppe of Baycu, hearing this, who (with his brother) governed the Normanes and Englishmen, little esteeming the power and riches of the west kingdome, unlesse by right of the Pope-dom, might largely rule all ye inhabitants of ye earth, he sendeth to Rome, he buyeth a palace, he seeketh out the senators, who with great gifts he given he joyneth with him in amitie, he sendeth for Hugh, Earle of Chester, and a great company, . . . and hartely prayeth them to goe with him to Italy . . . beyond the river of Poo. Pru-dent King William, when hee heard of such great prepara-tions. allowed not thereof, but thought it to be hurtfull to his kingdome, and many others, wherefore, he hastily saileth into England, and sodenly unlooked for in the Ile of Wight met with Odo the Bishoppe, and now desirous with great pompe to saile into Normandy, and there ye chiefest of his Realme being gathered together in the king's hall, the king spake in this sort. 'Excellent Peeres, hearken my wordes diligently, I beseech you give unto me your wholsome counsaile.

" 'Before I sailed over the Sea into Normandie I com-mended the government of England to my brother the Bishoppe of Bayou. . . .

" 'My brother hath greatly oppressed England and hath spoiled the Churches of their lands and rents, hath made tiem naked of the ornaments given by our predecessors, and hath seduced my knights and contemning me purposeth to traine them out beyond the Alpes, into foraine kingdomes,

Such was the Bishop of Bayeux, whilom owner of a great portion of the land registered in Domesday Book as Swindon. His history reveals what will now appear a strange state of matters. When Swindon was in its infancy eight centuries ago, a bishop commanded an army, and plundered a cathedral, than which two things it would be impossible to name others more opposed to what is at present considered the mission of a clerical dignitary. Moreover, he was the "count whom I set over my kingdom." Here is a bishop, a count, a general, and a robber, all in one. Could anything show more conclusively the confusion which followed close upon the Conquest?

an over great dolour grieveth my heart; especially for the Church of God, which he hath afflicted. . . . Consider you worthely what is to be done hereupon, and I beseech you insinuate it unto me.'

"And when all they fearing so great a performance doubted to pronounce sentence against him, the valian king saide, hurtfull rashnesse is alwaies to bee repressed . . .

"Now the king committed his said brother Odo to prizor, where he remained about ye space of foure yeers after, b wit, to the death of King William."

This is confirmed by Sappenberg, trans. Thorpe, in hs *History of England*, quoting from William of Malmesbuy and others.

Under the Bishop of Bayeux there were two
tenants; they were named Wadard, hence they
were probably related. Alured of Marlborough
also held land at Swindon. He seems to have
been a very extensive proprietor in North
Wilts at that date. One Uluric, too, owned
property here, and the fifth was Ulward, the
king's prebendary, whatever that may mean.
The lands registered as Swindon in Domesday
Book afterwards received distinctive names.
There was Haute, High, or Over Swindon,
Nether Swindon and Even Swindon. Haute,
High, or Over Swindon was undoubtedly upon
the hill. Over is a prefix not uncommonly
found before names of places indicating their
position to be over, or above that town whence
they drew their origin, or with which they
were connected. An instance is Overtown at
Wroughton, which still retains its name, and
whose position indicates its origin, being
situated high up upon the hill over-looking
Wroughton. Besides Haute, Nether, and
Even Swindon, there was Wicklescote, now
known as Westlecott. It may be observed
that north-east of Westlecott is a hill known as
Iscott hill. Cot comes from a Saxon word

meaning habitation, and is still preserved in cottage. It is probable that these two places—Westlecott and Iscott—have been the seat of habitations from the earliest times. Wicklescote afterwards belonged to persons of the names of Bluet and Bohun. Bohun is a name very celebrated in English History during the reign of Edward I. That monarch proceeded to tax both clergy and laity at his pleasure, heedless of the Great Charter, but was at length compelled by Humphrey Bohun and Roger Bigod,[1] two great noblemen, not only to

---

[1] Roger Bigod, fifth Earl of Norfolk, Marshall of England, born 1245, son of Hugh Bigod, justiciar. When called upon to serve in Gascony, while Edward took command in Flanders, he refused.

"By God, earl, you shall either go or hang."

"By God, O king, I will neither go nor hang."

The Council broke up, and Bigod and Bohun were joined by more than thirty of the great vassals. In answer to a general levy of the military strength, the two earls refused to serve in their offices of marshall and constable, and were therefore deprived of them.

When Edward sailed for Flanders, leaving the Prince in charge, they made the most of their opportunity, and protested boldly against exactions, being joined by the citizens of London. An assembly of the magnates and knights of the shires was called, Bigod and Bohun appeared in arms, the prince was obliged to confirm the charters.

Upon the return of the king the earls demanded of him

confirm that charter, but to add a clause to it by which it was provided that the nation should never in future be taxed without the consent of Parliament, a wise enactment which has secured the property of the subject against the rapacity of rulers, and also proved the foundation of England's wealth. All honour to the illustrious Humphrey Bohun.

Wicklescote was then held under the manor

a confirmation in person, to which after long hesitation he yielded.

After this, and the death of Bohun in 1298, Bigod's power seems to have collapsed.

    1301.   He made the king his heir, and gave up his marshall's rod.

    1302.   Surrendered his lands and title, receiving them back intail.

A chronicler ascribes this surrender to a quarrel between Roger and his brother John.

    1306.   Bigod died without issue, and in consequence of his surrender his dignities vested in the crown.

He married twice :—

    1. Alina, daughter and co-heir of Philip Basset, chief justiciar of England in 1261, and widow of Hugh le Despenser, chief justiciar of the barons.

    2. Alice, daughter of John of Hainault.

Humphrey Bohun, fourth Earl of Hereford, son of Bigod's colleague, took an active part in opposing the Despensers and Edward II. He was killed at Boroughbridge, 1322. A Bohun held the Basset lands.—*Dictionary of National Biography.*

of Wootton Bassett. Later, in the reign of
Edward III., who occupied the throne from
1327 to 1377, the Everards and Lovells were
proprietors. A Katherine Lovell, seemingly
in the reign of Henry IV. (1399 to 1413), gave
certain lands at Wicklescote to Lacock Abbey,
which, at the dissolution of monasteries—which
took place in the year 1535—were bought by
John Goddard, Esq., of Upper Upham. Sir
Edward Darell, of Littlecote, near Hungerford,
had lands here in the early part of the reign of
Edward VI. John Wroughton had the manor
in the seventh year of Henry VI., that is,
in 1429.

The manor of High Swindon was conferred
by King Henry III. (reigned from 1216 to
1272) upon a relation of his, in fact, his half-
brother, William de Valence, the celebrated
Earl of Pembroke, of Goderich Castle. His
son, Aylmer de Valence, held it in the year
1323. Valence is a name familiar to the
readers of Sir Walter Scott's novels. Aylmer
de Valence, it will be remembered, is the hero
or one of the principal characters in *Castle
Dangerous* ; and is there represented as the
nephew of the Earl of Pembroke. The widow

of Aylmer de Valence held the manor in 1377.
She was known as Mary de St. Paul, Countess
of Pembroke, and her memory has been per-
petuated in consequence of her having founded
Pembroke Hall, Cambridge. Aylmer de Valence having died without issue, part of the
estate fell to the daughter of his sister, Elizabeth Comyn. She married Richard, second
baron Talbot of Goderich Castle, who thus
became owner of this part of Swindon. The
Talbots were a celebrated family. Shakespeare has immortalised the name in one of his
historical dramas. Later, in 1473, it belonged
to John, Earl of Shrewsbury. At this date the
manor was held under what was known as the
Honor of Pont'large.[1] At length, in the year
1560, the estate was purchased by Thomas
Goddard, Esq., of Upham, ancestor of the
present owner, A. L. Goddard, Esq.

Phillip Avenell had landed property at Swindon in the time of Edward I. He held it
under the Abbess of Wilton. The names of
Avenell, Spilman, and Everard are found here
about 1316 A.D.

---

[1] Or Pont de l'Arche.

Olivia [1] Basset, wife of Hugh Despenser—a distinguished name—had an estate at Swindon in the seventh year of Edward I., that is, in 1279. The grandson [2] of this Olivia Basset married Eleanor, co-heir of Gilbert de Clare, Earl of Gloucester. [3] In the thirty-third year of the burly monarch, Henry the Eighth, a Wenman owned the estate known as Even Swindon. The Abbey of Malmesbury, the Monastery of Ivychurch, and later, the Everards and Alworths also held portions of these lands, which were originally in the hands of only five proprietors. The Wenman family seem to have purchased their property here about 1541, or soon after the dissolution of monasteries. At the same time, Sir Thomas Bridges bought some lands at Swindon. He was the ancestor of the Duke of Chandos. In the days of the Virgin Queen Elizabeth the woods, "super Rectoriam," were purchased from the Crown by Thomas Stephens, of Burderop. The Viletts also held landed property at Swin-

---

[1] Her name is also given as Oliva, or Aliena.
[2] Hugh Despenser, junior
[3] Hence the " Coate of Clare."

don; the family is now (1866) represented by Mrs. Rolleston, of the Square, Swindon.

At the present day (1866) the largest landed proprietor of Swindon is A. L. Goddard, Esq. He also owns the estate known as Broome. This, in the reign of Edward I., belonged to the priory of Martigny. Afterwards, at the dissolution of the monasteries, it came into the possession of the Seymours, an ancient and widespread family. Later it descended through Katherine, the daughter of Charles, sixth Duke of Somerset, to the Wyndhams of the Egremont house; from whom it was purchased by the present owner. When Aubrey, the widefamed Wiltshire antiquarian, came to Swindon about two centuries ago, he seems to have visited Broome, since he alludes to it in the following passage :—

" Mem.—At Brome, near Swindon, in a pasture ground, near the house stands up a great stone, q. Sarsden,[1] called Longstone, about 10 feet high, more or less, which I take to be the remayner of a Druidish Temple ; in the ground below are many stones in a right line, thus : O O O O O O O."

[1] The etymology of this word is uncertain. Aubrey

The stone seems to have disappeared, but to this day the field is known as Longstone field. There still remain a number of Sarsdens scattered about, but without any apparent attempt at order. A similar stone is said to have once stood in Burderop Park, about a mile further. Whether Aubrey was right or wrong in his conjecture concerning the Druidical origin of the assemblage of stones which he saw, it is now of course impossible to tell, unless some fortunate discovery should throw light upon the matter. It may be remarked that on the slope of the field known as Brud-hill—some say

derives it from Sarsden (Cesar'sdene?) a village three miles from Andover. Other suggestions are A. S. selstan = great stone. A. S. sar = grievous, stan = a stone. A. S. sesan = rocks. Sarsens or sarsdens are also known as grey wethers or Druid stones.—*Hunter*.

Canon Jackson comments : "Of the great stones mentioned by Aubrey none are now remaining." Mr. Morris says : "I resolved on finding out, if possible, what had become of 'the remayner of a Druidish Temple,' and after some years I was rewarded for my trouble by making the discovery that the stones were actually sold to the Waywardens of Cricklade, and removed to that town, where they were broken up and used to make good the pitching in the streets. . . . If this was the use the Swindonians of old were prepared to make of 'the remayner of a Druidish Temple,' the world at large may feel thankful that they had no control over Stonehenge and Avebury."

Blood-hill, a name that would indicate fighting —adjoining the Park at Swindon, there is beside the footpath, a similar row of Sarsden stones to those seen at Broome by Aubrey, though these are much sunk in the earth.

The extent of Swindon, both during the Saxon times and for centuries after, was in all probability inconsiderable, that is, as a town. There were probably a few great mansions scattered here and there, the residences of the tenants under the great families, who from time to time owned the adjacent estates ; and near these the cottages of the labourers. The remains still existing of this period are so very inconsiderable that it is next to impossible to found even a probable conjecture upon them. A few years ago what was considered a Saxon arch or doorway was discovered in a cellar in High Street, and whilst making some excavations in the New Road, it was stated that the workmen came upon a Saxon pillar. Remains such as these must ever be liable to suspicion, there being no corroborative testimony in the shape of coins or similar articles. Saxon Swindon seems to have entirely disappeared ; nor has Norman Swindon met with any better

c

fate. Mediæval Swindon, may, perhaps, in a
certain sense, remain in a few scattered carvings
of no importance, but even these are doubtful.
It was not until Thomas Goddard, Esq., of
Upham, purchased the Swindon estate in 1560
that the place emerged from obscurity. The
Goddards then became the principal proprietors, and the leading family of the town,
and have remained so ever since—through a
period of three centuries.

Even during the Civil Wars Swindon seems
to have in a general sense escaped notice.
Both the Parliamentary forces and those of the
King must have marched within a few miles
of the place, if they did not pass through ; at
any rate it is not improbable that a detachment
came here. Just before the first battle of Newbury, which took place in 1644, the Earl of
Essex fell back before the King from Tewkesbury, surprised a Royalist garrison at Cirencester, and, continues Lord Clarendon, the
historian of the war : " From hence the Earl,
having no farther apprehension of the king's
horse, which he had no mind to encounter upon
the open campagne, and being at the least
twenty miles before him, by easy marches, that

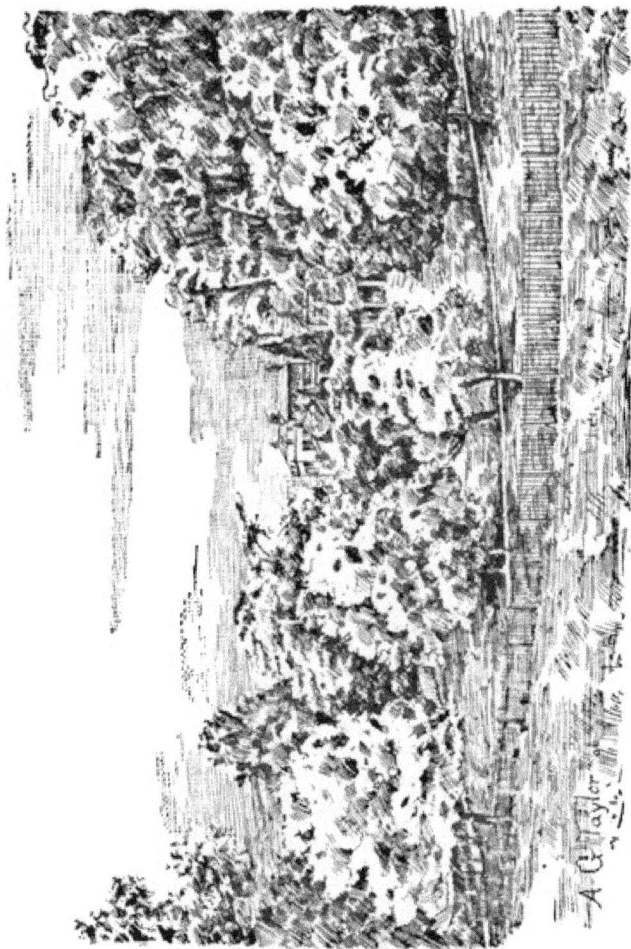

THE LAWN, SWINDON.
The Home of the Goddard Family.

his sick and wearied soldiers might overtake him, moved through that deep and enclosed country, North Wiltshire, his direct way to London," closely pursued by the King and Prince Rupert, who came up with the enemy about seven miles from Swindon, and an action ensued, which turned out in favour of the Royalists. If Swindon ever became the scene of civil contention it was probably when the two hostile armies passed by at such a small distance. Some few years since, while making excavations in the middle of Wood Street, just opposite Mr. Chandler's, the workmen came upon a number of human bones, amongst them a fine skull, which was preserved. A similar discovery was made in Cricklade Street. These remains may have had some connection with those unhappy times when England was divided against itself, but of course this is no more than a conjecture.

Shortly after the Civil War came to an end, Aubrey, the Wiltshire antiquary, visited Swindon, and has left the following cursory memorandum of its condition at that date :—

" Swindon. This towne probably is so called, quasi Swine-Down, for it is situated on

a hill or downe, as well as many other places,
viz., Horseley, Cow-ton, Sheep-ton, etc., take
their names from other animals.   It is famous
for the Quarrie, which is neer the Towne, of
that excellent paveing stone, which is not in-
ferior to the Purbec Grubbes, but whiter, and
will take a little polish; they send it to London;
it is a white stone ; it was not discovered until
about thirty years agon : and I am now writing
in 1672 : yet it lies not above 4 or 5 foot
deep.   Here is on Munday every weeke a
gallant Market for Cattle which encreased to
its now greatness upon the plague at Highworth, about 20 years since.

" Here, at Highworth, and so at Oxford, the
poore people, etc., gather the cow-shorne in the
meadows and pastures and mix it with hay, and
strawe, and clap it against the walles for ollit ;
they say 'tis good ollit, i.e., fuell : they call it
Compas, they meane I suppose, Compost.   All
the soil hereabout is a rich lome of a darke haire
colour."

It will be observed that Aubrey gives
Swindon anything but a dignified origin.
Aubrey, however, is by no means an infallible
authority.   Though an earnest, painstaking,

and often most intelligent antiquarian, he often displays a childishness—a gossiping disposition similar to that which made him labour so hard at the collection of ghost stories— which led him to adopt the first thought that occurred, without investigation, and to take up time and paper, in recording little peculiarities, like that of the "cow-shorne," which would have been much more usefully expended in giving an account of the condition of the place itself. Swine are not fed as a rule upon downs ;[1] when herds of swine were kept their chief haunts were the forest,—the boar's native home—where acorns, beech masts, and roots, can be found in abundance. Nor, although in later times Swindon has become celebrated for its pig market, could such a circumstance be regarded as having given rise to its name, for the simple reason that the market was not held until the middle of the seventeenth century, and the place is registered as Swindon[2] in Domesday Book, compiled towards the end of

[1] Mr. Jackson also questions Aubrey's derivation : A down is not suitable for fattening swine. More likely named from some owner, a Saxon or Danish " Sweyne," a name still well known in the county.

[2] Svindone or Svindune.

the eleventh century. Aubrey was probably misled by the sound. Swindon certainly does bear an affinity to Swine-don, when pronounced with the i long. There does not appear any other ground whatever for the conjecture, nor can this ground be admitted. Sweyn-dune is a far more reasonable conjecture.

Even at that date it seems Swindon was famous for its quarries. The stone was even sent to London. It may be remarked that the spring of water known as the Wroughton spring, it being just out of the town on the Wroughton road, was discovered upon making some excavations in search of stone in the adjoining field ; it is said not much over a century since. It is only necessary to take a glance at these quarries to see to what a wonderful extent they have been worked since their discovery some 200 years ago—a good and indisputable testimony to the quality of the stone. A few years back an interesting discovery to geologists was made in that quarry known as Tarrant's. It was a stem of a tree fossilized. Scarcely a mantlepiece in the town that was not furnished forthwith with a piece of this fossil tree, so great was the curiosity awakened by the

discovery, yet so much larger was the supply
than the demand, that two large logs, if such
an expression may be used, still remain in Mr.
Tarrant's yard, Sands, visible to all passers-by.

The "gallant Market" to which Aubrey
refers, still continues to be held, though under
very different auspices to those beneath which
it was then conducted. A magnificent building
now shelters corn dealers from the inclemencies
of the weather, while in a short time cattle
will be accommodated immediately without the
town. It appears from these cursory notes of
Aubrey that there was a cattle plague in the
country to ruin and intimidate farmers two
hundred years ago as well as now, or rather as
two years since. The market was held on the
same day then as now—Monday. This market
owes its existence to Thomas Goddard, a de-
scendant of the one who purchased the estate
at Swindon in 1560. Thomas Goddard, Esq.,
obtained a charter [1] to hold a weekly market,
and two fairs yearly in 1627, which said markets and fairs have been duly observed since in
the Square, Swindon. The custom to which

[1] This charter was printed in the *Swindon Advertiser*,
12th September, 1859.

Aubrey refers with respect to "cow-shorne"[1] at Highworth—if he means that it was used as fuel—is remarkable in one way, since a somewhat similar one obtains in Palestine, according to travellers—it might there be termed camel-shorne.

"What's one's bane is another's blessing," says the old proverb. The plague which harassed Highworth proved beneficial to Swindon, which seems to have escaped the ravages of the cattle disease as well in the seventeenth century as in the nineteenth. It would be interesting to learn the symptoms of that cattle disease which overran the country in the seventeenth century in order to compare it with that which so lately assumed so threatening an aspect. The market, established in 1627 by Thomas Goddard, Esq., was probably the making of Swindon. Henceforward it became indisputably a town. He seems to have been the only man in a course of eight centuries who showed anything approaching public spirit towards the place. The Goddard family very

---

[1] Shard or shorn, by some thought to be the derivation of Shakespeare's "shard-born beetle": *i.e.* bred in shard or dung [*Macbeth*] (Jackson).

early had a connection of some sort with
Swindon. The name is said to be found in
deeds relating to the parish so far back as the
year 1404—over four centuries ago. They
have been magistrates and members of Parliament for many generations.

The few preceding facts have been almost all
that it has been found possible to gather, which
in any way throw light upon the ancient state
of Swindon. It is from them, and from their
scarcity, very evident that the place was in old
times of very little importance as a town.
These facts, however few and meagre, are, it is
probable, all that will ever be found. Swindon,
it must be recollected, never boasted a monastery, nor was it ever made into a corporate
town. Many places which were once of importance sufficient to render a corporation
necessary—such as Wootton Bassett—are now
declining, or at a standstill, whilst Swindon, less
favoured in days gone by, is rapidly expanding
and developing its resources. Still, however
modern may be its importance, a town that can
date from before the Conquest—back to the
days of the Danes and the famous Sweyn, can
never be despised in point of antiquity.

CHAPTER II

ALTHOUGH Swindon had no monastery, yet it had a church from the earliest times, known as Holyrood, or more familiarly spoken of as the "Old Church" to distinguish it from the new; for Holyrood, as a place of worship, is a thing of bygone days. The bells are silent, the belfry itself has disappeared, and of the body of the church, only the chancel and two ancient ivy-covered arches remain. There were no literary monks at Swindon in the mediæval ages to leave behind them a curious chronicle for the learned of to-day to decipher —letter by letter and sentence by sentence— but there is the churchyard record with its ever-open pages, all saying the same thing, though in so many different ways; tombstones and tablets with many a tale of times gone by traced upon them. Here are no gaily-decorated manuscripts, but here is the handwriting of

RUINS OF HOLYROOD CHURCH, SWINDON.

death, and its emblazonry of cross-bones, urns,
and praying figures.   Not a step can be taken
through this ancient churchyard that does not
tread upon those who have lived and died, and
disappeared ; scarce a turf can be turned without bringing to light the melancholy and mouldering remains of mortality.   Here the awful
line of the poet Young is literally true—

" Where is the dust that has not been alive ? "

Look at the rank, tall grass, damp even at
noonday ; its roots are nourished by that which
once gaily trod the grass of its day under foot.
Look at the dark green moss upon the tombstones—shortly it will fill up and hide the last
memorial of those who lie beneath ; others
there are which have sunk out of sight in the
same earth which received those they were intended to commemorate—such is the end of
man.   Even the graven stone cannot perpetu-
ate his memory—he dies, and his place knows
him no more.   Verily this is the home of the
dead.

Why did our ancestors erect their sacred
buildings so near their mansions ?   Here is the
churchyard actually coming up to the very wall

of the house. The same thing may be observed at Lydiard Tregoze, the seat of Lord
Bolingbroke, where the church and the manor
house almost touch. Probably priestly influ-
ence had something to do with it—the present
generation would scarcely be gratified with the
view of funerals being conducted beneath their
very windows. To-day men appear to endea-
vour to become fearless of death by placing it
out of sight, rather than by familiarising themselves with its accompaniments—probably on
the theory that familiarity breeds contempt.
The appearance of Holyrood Church, so far as
it is possible to judge from descriptions and
drawings, must have been very venerable,
though it had not the slightest pretension to
architectural beauty. The tower, which was
square and dwarfed, as if left unfinished, and
much overgrown with ivy, stood at the western
end and opposite the chancel. On the northern
side was a kind of transept. The pillars which
supported the nave are of a rather unusual
shape, sexagonal. The two arches which remain have a very ancient appearance, increased
by the ivy which encircles them. That portion
which has been preserved is simply the chan-

cel. It originally was in the possession of the
Rolleston family, who were under an obligation
to keep it in repair, but upon the demolition
of the ancient edifice and the completion of
Christ Church—the present place of worship—
they transferred their rights to the new building, and the parish undertook the charge of
maintaining the old church. The old church
having been found inadequate to accommodate
the constantly increasing population of Swindon, it was proposed to enlarge and restore it,
and the committee appointed for that purpose
had agreed to recommend to the parish the
adoption of a design by the celebrated architect,
Mr. Gilbert Scott, for that purpose. The late
Mr. Goddard, however, offering a new site,[1]
and his son, Mr. A. L. Goddard, promising a
donation[2] towards the building, the parish, at a
vestry meeting, decided to erect a new church
on another site. The donation of Mr. Goddard
formed the nucleus of a building fund, the liber-
ality of the parishioners and the indefatigable
exertions of the Rev. H. G. Baily, the vicar,
among his friends, providing the remainder of

[1] This included ground for a new churchyard.
[2] £100.

the money. The total cost of the church was
£8,000. Mr. Baily[1] worked with great energy,
and he had a large share in obtaining for his
parish the beautiful edifice known as Christ
Church.[2] The Diocesan Society of that day
refused any grant because the living was not in
the patronage of the bishop, and the Incorpo-
rated Church Building Society were only able
to give £130. The materials of the old church,
save the chancel, which was preserved, were
sold to assist the fund for erecting the new
edifice. The bells (the tenor was cracked and
re-cast) were removed to the new church, and
are those now in the Parish Church.

Holyrood was not the original designation
of the church. In the fourteenth century—and
very early in it, 1302—it was dedicated to St.
Mary. About fifty years after this date, or in
the year 1359, the vicarage was first endowed.
The monastery of Wallingford had a certain
interest in the place, the monks having a pen-
sion, which was taken out of the rectorial tithes.
Before the dissolution of monasteries — that

---

[1] The Rev. H. G. Baily, after nearly forty years' work in
Swindon, accepted the Rectory of Lydiard Tregoze, in the
gift of Lord Bolingbroke.   [2] 1850.

great blow which was dealt in 1535 to the
Roman Catholic religion—the Priory of St.
Mary, Southwick, had the rectory. Hence it
will be seen that although no monastery was
ever in existence at Swindon, it had, through
its church, connection with several of those
great nurseries of the Catholic faith. The
Abbey of Malmesbury, the Nunnery of Wilton,
the Monastery of Ivychurch, near Sarum or
Salisbury, the Monastery of Wallingford, and
lastly the Priory of Southwick, had all, to a
more or less degree, some interest in Swindon,
whose ancient inhabitants were therefore doubtless well acquainted with the cowl and its customs. It may be remarked that after a lapse
of many centuries the Catholic faith has once
again begun to make headway in Swindon as
well as in other localities—there being a Roman
Catholic chapel in Bridge Street, New Swindon,
which is quite a modern erection. England
is beginning to feel the effects of universal
toleration—a great problem which is working
itself out around us, and has in America arrived
at such startling developments.[1]

[1] It must be remembered that this was written in 1867,
soon after the Civil War.

After the dissolution of the monasteries, the rectory fell, about the year 1560, into the hands of the Stephen family, then resident at Burderop. It continued in their hands until 1584, when it was purchased from them by the Vilett family.

At least one distinguished man has been Vicar of Swindon. This was no less a person than Narcissus Marsh, who afterwards became Archbishop of Armagh.[1] He does not appear, however, to have been a vicar for a longer period than one year, which was 1662. Swindon has not been noticeable as a prolific place for remarkable men.[2] It certainly never had the chance which other places had. There was no monastery to collect or focus the learning and ability of the neighbourhood. Let not then the soil of Swindon be despised on that account. "Blame the culture, not the soil," as Horace puts it. The non-existence of a monastery cannot be too much lamented by the antiquarian.[3]

---

[1] Canon Jackson notes : "In the list of Vicars are three peculiar names—Milo King, Aristotle Webbe, and Narcissus Marsh."

[2] Richard Jefferies himself appears the only literary man of note produced in this locality. (Ed.)

[3] In his interesting *Swindon Fifty Years Ago*, Mr. Wil-

Holyrood Church must have seen some strange changes in that long course of five hundred years. Could the stones speak, what stories might they not tell of times gone by— of armed men, of the knights who fought in the Wars of the Roses ; later, of the quaintly cut beards and curiously slashed garments of Queen Elizabeth's reign ; of the careless cavaliers of King Charles's days ; of monks and mass superseded by surpliced clergymen and their comparatively modern service. The bells —what changes they must have rung :

> "For full five hundred years I've swung
>   In my old gray turret high,
> And many a changing theme I've rung
>   As the time went stealing by"

might have been traced upon them. But the stones are dumb, save the records of the dead ; the bells are no longer heard, the belfry is down. The jackdaws have lost their building

liam Morris devotes two chapters to local "Worthies," amongst whom are Dr. G. A. Mantell, Mr. James Strange, William Pike, etc. But as, with the exception of Robert Sadler, they are literally *local* worthies, they need not be enumerated here, as Jefferies' statement is at present irrefutable.

place, though they still remain in numbers in
the neighbourhood, and may be seen any day
in the adjacent park. There was a very
general feeling of regret when the old place
was discovered to be doomed. " I have completed a monument more lasting than marble,
more durable than brass," sang Horace on
finishing a book, and his words have been
fulfilled. So, though Holyrood has gone,
there yet remains a record, slight and scanty,
but still a record, written upon that apparently
most perishable material, paper. Aubrey, who
has already been referred to as visiting Swindon about two centuries ago, did not forget
the church. Here is his memoranda concerning it :—

" Church. In the church is nothing observ-
able left in the windowes except in the first,
on the south side of the chancell, viz., the
coate of Clare. This cross is on a tombe
about a foote higher than the pavement on
the north side of the aisle, belonging to ——
Goddard, Esq. . . . In the same aisle,
beneath his picture, was buried, aged 25,
1641, Thomas Goddard, Esq., husband of
Jane, daughter to Edmund Fettiplace, Knight.

his coate thus, Goddard (diagram). Somebody
is buried by. I suppose his wife, but the inscription is not legible. This on an old free-
stone in the chancell, now worne out, Grubbe
of Poterne (sinister). Also Stephens of Burthorp. The same in other colours and metalls.
Near this lye buried two children of William
Levet, Esq. They were buried 1667.

" This under the altar, viz : " Here lieth the
body of Thomas Vilett, Gent. He departed
this life the 6th day of November, 1667. On
both sides lye buried his two wives.' .   .   .

" At the upper end of the church this inscription : ' Christus, qui mortuus est ut per
mortem suam superans mortem triumpharet,
a mortuis ad vivos exsuscitabit. Buried the
5th of June, An. Dom. 1610, the body of
Elenor Huchens, the wife of Thomas Huchens
of Ricaston. Shee to this parish twenty pound
gave to the relief of the poore, the use for
ever. James Lord, and Henry Cus, her husbands, twenty pounds each of them gave to
the poore of this parish, the use for ever.'

" This in the chancell : ' Hic jacet Henricus
Alworth in hac vicinia natus, qui adolescentiam
in Schola Wintoniensi juventutem in Academia

Oxoniensi senectutem in Patria Wiltoniensi, feliciter consecravit, ubique, castè, sobriè, piè, sibi parcus, suis, beneficus, egenis effusus, ab omnibus desideratus, Obijt XVI die Augusti 1669 Ætatis suæ 75.' "

The first remark that Aubrey makes is, that there was in his time but little left in the windows—by the use of which expression he would seem to intimate that there once had been something in them. Now the date at which he passed through Swindon was but a short time after the conclusion of the Civil War, and it is well known that the soldiers of Cromwell's army had a great fancy for smashing everything which in their diseased and heated imaginations they conceived to bear what was called "the mark of the beast," that is, to savour of Rome. Like the iconoclasts of the continent they had a mad hatred of anything approaching an image. May it not then be reasonably conjectured that the Parliamentarian soldiers destroyed whatsoever they possibly could in a hasty visit to Swindon—such as might have occurred when the army of Essex passed through North Wilts in 1644? Aubrey himself, if we remember aright, mentions in another part of his work that such had been their conduct at Bishopstone church—perhaps five miles from Swindon—where they had smashed the stained glass, and left nothing for him to copy. Why may not the same thing have happened at Swindon? The windows themselves have gone since Aubrey's time, saving one which remains at the eastern extremity of the chancel, in which there is a little, but a very little, stained glass.[1]

It was the custom of the Roundheads to stable their horses in the old buildings which had once witnessed the celebration of mass— it is to be hoped no such desecration ever occurred in Holyrood.

Aubrey observed the "coate of Clare," that is, the arms of that house, in the first window on the south side of the chancel. In the time of Edward I., about 1279, one Olivia Bassett, as has been already mentioned, held lands at Swindon; and her grandson formed a matrimonial alliance with Eleanor, the co-heiress of

[1] Jefferies here, somewhat inconsistently, gives credence to the current traditions of Roundhead irreverence—the Parliamentarian army acting as a convenient scapegoat for the sacrilegious acts of contemporaries.

Gilbert de Clare, Earl of Gloucester, which perhaps may in some way throw light upon this "coate of Clare" which Aubrey saw.[1] "Stephens of Burthorp" would mean Stephens of Burderop. Burderop is understood, like Swindon, to have been named by the Danes, thorp being a Danish word for village. This lends strength to the supposition that Swindon was named from Sweyn, since it shows that the Danes had settlements in the neighbourhood. Levet—two children of which name Aubrey found were buried here 1667—is an ancient name, and persons of that designation long had some connection with the place. It is said that the name Levet or Leviet occurs in the Domesday Survey of Swindon. Alworth is also an ancient name, and one early found here. The Viletts then, as now, occupied the chancel. It may be observed that Aubrey gives no inscriptions whatever earlier than the century in which he lived—that is, dated before the commencement of the seventeenth century. Between 1600 and 1700 there are numerous interments commemorated with a tombstone and inscription, but earlier than

[1] See chap. i., p. 14.

that there does not appear to be any. Those
that Aubrey copied, though ancient now, were
most of them modern in his time, two hundred years ago, yet the church has been in
existence full five hundred years. The truth
would appear to be that it is only within the
last two centuries and a half that Swindon
has become the residence of persons wealthy
enough to commemorate their losses by the
aid of the engraver's expensive art. Such
men as Odin the Chamberlain, the Bishop of
Bayeux, the Earl of Pembroke, the Earl of
Shaftesbury, the Talbots, and the Darells of
Littlecot, no doubt had their family vaults
elsewhere; and with the solitary exception of
the "coate of Clare" not a memorial of the
noble families once connected with Swindon
seems to remain in the place. After 1560,
when the estate came into the Goddard family,
and the adjoining mansion became the residence of the owners, the church was made the
sepulchre of persons whose memory was per-
petuated by tombs and inscriptions.

The dimensions of the old church were as
follows: The tower was in length 18 feet 2
inches, the nave 60 feet 1 inch, the chancel 31

feet 6 inches, altogether 109 feet 9 inches.
The breadth of the north aisle was 16 feet 5
inches, the nave 21 feet 5 inches, and the south
aisle also 16 feet 5 inches, making a total
breadth of 54 feet 3 inches, while the height
of the nave was 30 feet. It was, therefore, a
structure of some considerable size. The body
of the church, which has now disappeared,
contained a number of tablets, some near the
pillars, others around the walls. Those adjacent to the three pillars of the south aisle were
in memory of William Harding, 1821 ; Gulielim Horne, 1730 ; Hannah Nobes, 1807; Rev.
John Neate, 1719 ; James Bradford, 1829 ; and
the Rev. Edmund Goodenough, 1807. Upon
and within the south wall of the church were
affixed the following : To John Skull, 1755 ;
Edmund Goddard, 1776 ; Joseph Randall,
1768 ; Millicent Neate, 1764 ; and Thomas
Goddard Vilett, 1817. On or near to the
pillars of the north aisle were originally affixed
monuments to Elizabeth Slack, 1789 ; Rev.
John William Aubrey, 1806 ; Mary Broadway,
1747 ; Francis Miles, 1834 ; Richard Wayt,
1746 ; Ann Yorke, 1807 ; John Smith, 1775 ;
and Henry Herring, 1767. Adjacent to the

wall upon the north side were tablets to John Goddard, 1678; Richard Goddard, 1732; Ambrose Goddard, 1815; Gulielim Gallimore, 1697; Thomas Wayt, 1753; Hannæ Tubb, 1756; and Elizabeth Evans, 1763. These were carefully removed upon the destruction of the building, and the majority of them are still to be seen preserved in the chancel.

The stone-paved walk from the Planks up to the chancel is in a great measure composed of gravestones. One may be observed upon the right hand immediately before the entrance, upon which there is cut a simple cross without inscription or date that can be seen—which is perhaps even more suitable than a fulsome epitaph contradicting its own purpose by a superabundance of adjectives. The chancel is at present almost completely full of tablets and other monuments of the dead, many having been removed here from the body of the church. Over the high arched doorway within may be seen several gloomy hatchments, the monuments of departed greatness, with the usual inscriptions, such as " Resurgam." Against the wall leans the royal arms detached from its original position ; while upon the elevation afforded by the steps which once approached the altar stand the unused reading-desk and carved communion table. The air is damp and cold, the light dim and gloomy—it is silent, deserted, a fit resting-place for the dead, or for meditation. Here no longer is heard the voice of the warning preacher, no longer rises the hymn of thanksgiving, no longer is received the cup of commemoration; it is a place of tradition, the dwelling-place of the spirit of the past. A church must ever be a place of gloom to the majority of mankind, but a church which is deserted has its gloom deepened tenfold. It seems as though men had deserted that hope with which they formerly reinvigorated themselves within it.

At the east end, beneath the window, is the following inscription upon a stone let in even with the pavement: " Here lieth the body of Anne Vilett, wife of Thomas Vilett, gent., and daughter of Edmund Webb, of Rodbourne, Esqure, who departed this life December 6, 1643. Her age 54. She had living of eight children only one." The arrangement of the inscription upon this stone, as well as upon the two following, is peculiar, and at first sight

hardly intelligible; the graver would seem to
have been at a loss how to cut out what he
was required without crowding, The stone
close by has the following inscription : " Here
lieth the body of Thomas Vilett, gent. Hee
departed this life the 6th day of November
1667 ; also Captn. John, son of ye Sd. Ths.
Vilett, who died March ye 17, 1700, aged 70
years." The first part of this inscription is the
same as that which Aubrey saw and copied
when he visited this place two centuries since ;
that relating to the son, Captain John, has
been added since his time. The third stone
is in memory of Thomas Vilett's second wife,
whose memory is preserved in these words :
" Aug, 24, 1650, was buried Martha, second
wife of Thomas Vilett, gent., and daughter
of Thomas Goddard Esqure. She had three
children livinge." All three of these stones,
besides the inscriptions, have devices graven
upon them. On the south wall of the church is
a monument to three sisters : Mary, widow of
John Broadway, whilom Vicar of the parish,
died Jan. 7, 1747, leaving £20 yearly to the
poor of the Parish ; Dorothy Brind died 1748 ;
and Margaret Brind died the same year, leav-

ing £100 to the poor of the parish. A tablet
on the same wall records some benefactions, of
the interest of £100, given by one Horne;
Joseph Cooper in 1790 gave some lands at
Stratton St. Margaret, in lieu of and augmen-
tation of the same. Near this is a very ancient
and curious tablet which was seen and copied
by Aubrey, but the peculiar spelling of which
renders it sufficiently interesting to be copied
verbatim. It runs thus : " Bvryed 5 of Ivne,
the body of Elenor Hvchens the wife of
Thomas Hvchens of Ricaston. Shee of this
parish : 20 povnds gave to the releefe of the
poor, the vse for ever. James Lorde and
Henry Cvs her hvsbandt, 20 povnd each of
them gave to the poor of this parish the vse
for ever " (v. page 35).

On the north wall there is a small tablet to
the memory of Elizabeth Evans, dated 1763,
which appears to have once stood in the body
of the church. The inscription contains a
memorandum of a rather singular gift, yet no
doubt very acceptable to the recipients : " By
her will bearing date IX day of May 1763 she
bequeathed £50 to repair pews of this Church
and also the interest of £70 to purchase six

gowns to be given yearly in St Thomas' day
to six poor women inhabitants of this parish,
whose age shall exceed 60 years." The Vilett
family appear to have occupied the chancel;
the Goddard vaults are immediately without
the remaining portion of the building, on the
north side between it and the mansion. The
number of interments is evident from the large
space covered by the stones, one of which has
graven upon it a curious figure, apparently of a
person in a long robe, praying. The following
is an inscription upon a tablet erected in 1838 :
" Near this place lie the remains of Ambrose
Goddard, Esq., and of Sarah Marva, his wife.
They lived nearly forty years in the adjacent
mansion, happy in the love of each other, and
in promoting the happiness of all around them,
though severely tried by the loss of many of a
numerous family. He represented the county
of Wilts in Parliament 35 years, honestly and
faithfully, seeking no reward but the testimony
of his own conscience and the esteem of his
constituents. His wife was highly gifted, and
a bright example of Christian grace. They
both endeavoured to serve God, by doing good
to man. Through the merits of Christ may

their services be accepted, and their happiness protracted in a blessed eternity."

" A. Goddard, died June, 1815, S. M. Goddard, April, 1818. This tablet was erected by their few surviving children as a memorial of their gratitude and affection."

The Goddards have now sat in Parliament over half a century. It has been remarked of the present head of that family that he is never absent when there is any likelihood of a division to require his vote. Their policy has ever been a consistent Conservatism.

One of the tablets originally upon the north wall of the body of the church exhibited the following inscription : " Here lieth the body of John Goddard, gent, died December, 1678." This one may still be seen. It is in memory of John Vilett, Esqr. : " Deo optimo maximo. Hoc Sacravium instauravit et exoruavit Johannes Vilett armiger, A.D. 1736."

Another was in memory of Thos. Smyth, D.D., died 1790, aged 86 ; of whom it was recorded that he was vicar of the parish ; also to Mrs. Jane Smyth, who died in 1787 at the age of 74 ; they having lived happily together for a period of nearly half a century. But the

most extraordinary monument is that in
memory of one William Noad, and his four
wives. Hannah, his first, died in 1733, aged
28 years ; Hannah II., died in 1741, aged 29 ;
Martha, the third, died 1766, at the age of 62 ;
, Ann, the fourth, died in 1776, aged 54 years ;
and finally, William Noad died himself in the
year 1781, aged 70. This Noad, one might
imagine, was a Mahommedan at least, since he
managed to have the solacement of as many
wives as is allowed by the Koran to the followers of the prophet, and a clever fellow, too,
to steer clear of bigamy. Four wives—this is
the "Wife of Bath" reversed. If any one
understood what matrimonial life is, one would
think this Noad must have done so. What a
pity he did not write his memoirs for the guid-
ance of future husbands ! He died at length at
the allotted age of man—three score years and
ten—which fact shows what may be done in a
lifetime. Noad must have known a good deal
about womankind. His occupation in life was
that of clerk of the parish. Altogether William
Noad may be regarded as one of the most
extraordinary men Swindon ever produced. It
does not seem recorded that any such feat was

ever performed before or after. Probably we shall never see his like again. Peace be to his ashes, for it is to be feared he had little during his lifetime.

The office of clerk of the parish seems to have been for a long time hereditary in the Noad family. William Noad comes first, dying 1781; Henry Noad occupied the same post in 1752; another Henry Noad, in 1790, and a third Henry Noad vacated the office by death in 1848. This last Henry Noad is recorded to have held it for the extraordinary term of 57 years, or over half a century. What births, marriages, and deaths he must have recorded—the population of the place would in that time be almost entirely changed, a generation would pass away and another spring up, and he, clerk still, apparently stationary. The Noad family has been rather a remarkable one. The name is still known in Swindon. Cooper Noad, of Newport Street, makes good barrels, and challenges the world to produce better. All honour to the name of Noad!

Swindon seems to be a remarkably healthy situation, since some of the inhabitants have reached ages which might fairly be put into comparison with those of more widely-renowned places. Henry Noad just referred to was clerk for 57 years, and there lie in Holyrood church-yard the remains of four persons, who, with another of the same, only lately [1867], de-ceased, have not inaptly been designated the Five Patriarchs. The name of this remark-able assemblage of aged persons was Weekes. Thomas Weekes died in 1829, at the age of 91 years. Hannah Weekes, who departed this life in 1826, reached 82. Ed. Weekes, died 1821, aged 83. Susan in 1820, also 83 years of age ; while John Weekes, died 1866, reached the truly patriarchal age of 92 years. The sum of the lives of these five persons—all of whom, let it be observed, have died in the nineteenth century, and therefore it cannot be supposed that the virtue of Swindon air was better in the olden times than now—the sum amounts to 433 years! Eighty and six years was the average age of this remarkable family. Nor are they single examples of the remarkable longevity attained by the inhabitants of Swin-don. A lady of the name of Read (deceased during the present year) was, if we remember rightly, 91 years of age. Her remains were

E

interred at Wroughton. Mr. Shepherd, still living [1867], is another example—his age is 90. Mr. J. Jefferies has reached his eighty-fourth year. On the whole, Swindon can furnish examples of longevity which may challenge, if not defy, competition.

CHAPTER III

WHENEVER a man imbued with republican politics and progressionist
views, ascends the platform and delivers an
oration, it is a safe wager that he makes some
allusion at least to Chicago, the famous mush-
room city of the United States, which sprang
up in a night, and thirty years ago consisted
of a dozen miserable fishermen's huts, and now
counts over two hundred thousand inhabitants.
Chicago! Chicago! look at Chicago! and see
in its development the vigour which invariably
follows republican institutions. This is con-
founding the effect with the cause. The
hundreds of thousands of American emigrants

---

[1] Readers are reminded that this chapter has been left as
Jefferies wrote it, as, if it had been brought up to date,
much of the original matter must have been omitted as
obsolete ; whereas the details of thirty years ago are already
old enough to be interesting to the historian of the town.

must have something to do, and somewhere to
live.   Men need not go so far from their own
doors to see another instance of rapid expansion and development which has taken place
under a monarchical government.   The Swindon of to-day is almost ridiculously dispropor-
tioned to the Swindon of forty years ago.[1]
Houses have sprung up as if by enchantment,
trade has increased ; places of worship seem
constantly building to accommodate the ever
growing population ; as for public-houses, they
seem without number.   A whole town has
sprung into existence.   The expression New
Town is literally true.   It is new in every sense
of the word.   New in itself, new in the description of its inhabitants.   There was no republican form of self-government at Swindon forty
years ago—on the contrary, the place was
decidedly conservative, averse to change, and
looking at those who proposed it with suspicion.   It certainly was not owing to repub-
licanism that the place developed so fast.
That was not the cause, but that has been the
effect.   New Swindon is as decidedly demo-

---

[1] Middlesborough is another famous example of the rapid
growth of an English town.

cratic in its sentiments as Old Swindon was
conservative. The real cause of this enormous
development may be traced to that agent which
has effected an almost universal change—
Steam. Swindon is going ahead by steam—
the phrase is literally and metaphorically
correct. Yet the first push was not due to
steam. Forty-five years ago, or thereabouts,
the Wilts and Berks Canal came along close
below the Old Town, cutting right through
that flat meadow-land which was, twenty
years after, to resound with the hum of men.
The calm, contemplative, chew-a-straw steers-
man of the barge boats was then first seen
slowly gliding past, tugged along by a horse
walking on the tow-path. With what amaze-
ment and admiration the agricultural labourer's
children must have been struck as they viewed
the progress of the painted boat ; how they
must have envied such an apparently easy
life ! These children were designed to see
more astonishing things yet. Simple as they
were, they have seen in actual existence what
the wise men of former ages never dreamt of.
That part which it was found necessary for
the canal to pass through immediately beneath

Swindon was discovered to be the highest level on its whole course. Here there was no necessity for a lock for a distance of seven miles, and accordingly there is, at this day, a clear stretch of seven miles of water—New Swindon being situated somewhere about the middle, and consequently, a capital place to launch pleasure boats could the Canal Company be persuaded to speculate, or allow others to. A canal was something so utterly foreign in its conception to what the country people had been accustomed, that it was dubbed the " river," and goes by that name in the country round to this day. This long stretch of clear seven miles without a lock necessarily intercepted and received the water of numerous streams and rivulets, which—the right of use for certain periods of the year having been purchased by the Company—are used by them to keep this portion of the canal well filled, in order to supply the loss when a lock is opened. But so great was the traffic in those days, and accordingly so great was the quantity of water required, that it was discovered that in the summer, should it chance to be a dry one, there would always be the risk of a deficiency. Moreover, a lock might break, a bank might slip—a hundred possible accidents rendered a constant reservoir at this, the highest level desirable, and indeed necessary to the proper working of the canal. Accordingly the engineers of the Company cast about to find a fit place to construct a reservoir, and at last fixed on a valley at Coate, about a mile and a half from Swindon.

This valley was enclosed by a bank at each extremity, and the water of a brook which originally ran through it, together with that from other springs artificially compelled to run here, being allowed to accumulate, formed exactly what was desired; while the original course of the brook took off any superfluity that might occur from flooding, and by a branch from it · the canal could be always supplied. But the site offered one difficulty. There was a spring rising immediately without the upper bank of the reservoir, which it was found impossible to make run into it; moreover, it was wanted by the farmers and inhabitants of the vale beneath. This, then, must run under the reservoir. A brick culvert was accordingly constructed, but an unfortunate

oversight occurred. That part of the bottom
of the reservoir over which it was necessary
the culvert should be carried at the latter
end of its course, had originally been but one
remove from a morass, in short, was very
"shaky." Upon this unstable foundation the
culvert seems to have been placed, and with
the result which might have been anticipated.
The weight of the brick-work, with a superin-
cumbent load of earth and sand thrown on,
proved too great for the soft ooze upon which
it was placed. The culvert gradually sank in
places, the brickwork cracked, and leaks have
ever since been more or less frequent. One
occurred of a very serious character, when the
meadows below were flooded by the escaped
water of the reservoir, and had not a hatch
been beaten down by sledge hammers, it has
been thought that the reservoir bank must
have been washed away, and the thousands of
tons of water it contained would have been
precipitated into the vale, the effect of which
would have been an enormous damage to
property and probable loss of life. The reservoir, when full, covers an extent of seventy-two
acres, and is a favourite place for summer pic-

COATE RESERVOIR, SWINDON.

nics, being so near the town. Racing boats were formerly kept here, and some exciting pulls occurred, but this has long been discontinued. The want of boats—those that there are being utterly insufficient to supply the demand—causes much remark, since they would evidently be a paying speculation.[1] It is a beautiful sheet of water, approaching a mile in length, and has so much the appearance of being natural, that it is difficult even upon examination to consider it a work of man. The delusion is kept up by the numerous trees, and the romantic scenery around. The place was completed in 1822.

The completion of the canal—a wharf being of course constructed opposite Swindon—gave the first noticeable stimulus to the progress of the place. Swindon was a kind of junction, the canal here branching off into two—one going to Bristol, the other to Gloucester—and consequently a most favourable situation for trade. Coal now reached the town in greater quantities, and at a much less cost than previously, and a great carrying trade sprang up. Old inhabitants relate that in winter, when a

[1] This defect has long since been remedied.

sharp frost—somehow the frosty weather in these modern days never seems to come up to the description of that of yore—had bound the canal as if with iron, there was immediately an apprehension that the price of coals would rise ; which, if the frost continued, and the barges could not come up, it accordingly did, until all that remained upon the wharf being consumed, a coal famine would ensue. Enterprising farmers, whose teams could not work in that weather, would then dispatch a waggon and a trusty man even down to the very pit's mouth, purchase a load cheap, and make a good profit by retailing it around. These were the good old days! The poor must have suffered grievously for want of fuel when even the wealthy were straitened, especially in town, for in the country districts wood was plentiful, and the fireplaces adapted for consuming it. These were the halcyon days of the Canal Company. But a new wonder was to come and supplant the old.

Those who could afford to purchase a paper (for papers were not sold for half-pence then) and who could read it when they got it, had already been wondering over what would come

of that new invention—the steam engine. It
answered well to pump the water out of the
mines in Cornwall, boats had been propelled
by it, and finally, a tramway was constructed
at Manchester, which was found successful.
Then began the mania of railway speculation,
which, if it ruined thousands, proved the basis
upon which Swindon was to rise. The idea of
the Great Western Railway was at last started
—a gigantic scheme which was to connect the
two great cities of the South of England,
London and Bristol, by a level iron road.
Men were seen about in all directions, with
curious instruments, to the wonder of gaping
rustics, and the rage of farmers whose hedges
had gaps cut in them to clear the line of sight,
or whose property was trespassed upon by
enterprising engineers. The plan was looked
upon as monstrous by the aristocracy of the
country. These iron roads—who could hunt if
they intersected the land? These screaming
engines—where could be found a quiet corner
for the pheasants, if they were allowed to roam
across the country? Good-bye to the rural
retirement and peaceful silence of the deer-
dotted park, if once the white puff of the steam

engine curled over the ancient oaks! Great
opposition was offered to the railway bills, but
they were passed in spite of all, with a proviso
preserving parks; which, by the way, diverted
the Great Western from running immediately
by Old Swindon, it having been originally
designed to pass somewhere about where the
gasometer stands now, that is to say, to intrude
on the Goddard property.

The work was now vigorously proceeded
with. On the 26th of November, 1835, the
first contract was taken. This was the Wharn-
cliffe viaduct. Excepting about four miles in
the vicinity of London, the rest was let out
down to Maidenhead, during the following six
months. The work of the Bristol part was
commenced in 1836, and the first contract let
was a length of nearly three miles, extending
from the Avon to Keynsham. But the most
formidable undertaking on the whole line was
the celebrated Box tunnel. The shafts were
contracted for in the latter part of 1836, the
tunnel itself in the following year. Three long
years were expended in drilling—if such an
expression may be employed—this enormous
hole through the hill; it having not been

completed until 1841. The depth which the
shafts had to be sunk was on an average 240
feet, and their diameter is twenty-eight feet.
The tunnel is straight as a gun barrel, and can
be seen through from end to end, which allows
the observation of some singular effects of per-
spective. Its length is 3,200 yards, or nearly
two miles; it cost over half a million; no less
than 20,000,000 of bricks were employed in the
construction of the arching. The whole length
of the line from Paddington to Bristol is 118½
miles, and it was completed in the following
order:—Maidenhead opened up to, on June 4,
1838; Twyford, July 1,[1] 1839 ; Reading, March
30, 1840[2]; Steventon, June 1, 1840; Faringdon Road, July 20, 1840 ; Bristol to Bath,
August 31, 1840 ; Wootton Bassett Road,
December 17,[3] 1840; Chippenham, May 31,[4]
1841 ; to Bath, June 30, 1841. That part
of the line which runs past Swindon is for
several miles remarkably straight. Approaching Swindon from London, the rail is carried
through a deep cutting, especially near Stratton St. Margaret ; but upon the other side

[1] Or 5th.   [2] Another date is 6th April.
[3] Or 16th.   [4] Or 1st June.

it is raised upon an embankment. Much of
the earth of the embankment was taken from
a field on the slope of Kingshill Hill, at the
top of the Sands, Swindon; the soil being
purchased, of course, from the owner for that
purpose. A tramway was constructed in such
a manner that the trucks running down the
hill drew up a string of empty ones—a simple
but dangerous proceeding which gave rise to
one accident at least. It is to the railway that
Swindon owes its importance, and New Swindon its existence. Swindon now became the
emporium of North Wilts and the adjacent
counties. When it became a junction, and all
trains were ordered to stop here ten minutes,
it derived additional importance, and became a
place well-known to travellers. The station is
itself a fine building, and contains some large
refreshment rooms.

At length it was announced that a factory
was to be built for the manufacture of engines,
and other requisites of a railroad. This was
a good time for landed proprietors at New
Swindon. Land which was scarcely worth
the trouble of attending to, much of it covered
with furze, the retreat of rabbits and game, and

playground for boys, was purchased at a price
equal to that given for the best in other situa-
tions. One or two persons made fortunes. Up
rose the factory, and workmen began to pour in
from all quarters. Houses were built at a rate
which astonished the country, and a new class
of men, hitherto unknown in the neighbourhood, appeared, men who worked hard, earned
high wages, and were determined to live upon
the best they could afford. The agricultural
labourer was content with bread and beer,
the mechanic must have meat, groceries, and
other comforts.[1] The farm labourer bought
a smock-frock twice in his lifetime, and used
his grandfather's gaiters ; the mechanic dressed
smartly. Tradesmen found New Swindon
a profitable place — a Wiltshire California.
Publicans discovered that steel filings make
men quite as thirsty as hay dust. Moreover,
the mechanic must lodge somewhere. To
accommodate the constantly increasing number
of workmen it employed, the company built a
place, since known as the Barracks, upon the

---

[1] A characteristic feature of New Swindon, worthy of
notice in this connection, is the dearth of book-shops.

plan of French lodging - houses, to have a
common kitchen and common entrance, with
a day and night porter; but the thing did
not answer, and there stands the Barracks to
this day [1867], a great pile of buildings with
broken windows, the few inhabitants of which
were so dirty in their habits, that a year ago
[1866] it was thought to threaten a visitation
of cholera, and underwent a thorough clearing
under the supervision of the police. The
Briton likes to be independent, or what he
thinks so. Streets sprang up in all directions.
The situation was flat and damp, and there
was a deficiency of good water—it did not
matter; the mechanic must have a house, and
a house he had. The company built a church
and a Mechanics' Institute. The Dissenting
community have not been behindhand, and
chapels of almost every denomination may be
found. Persons of middle age describe the
change which has taken place since they can
remember as something almost incredible.
Streets stand where were formerly meadows
and hedgerows. Bridge Street contained two
residences. The one was what was considered
the manor house—it is now occupied by Mr.

Charles Hurt, and stands at the top of Bridge
Street on the right hand—the other was a
small cottage, a little further down towards
the canal. The cottage can still be seen—a
strange contrast with its thatched roof, dark
with age, and half hidden by weeds, to the
red-bricked and slated erections adjoining.
Bridge Street now contains three places of
worship, — a Methodist Chapel, a Roman
Catholic, and a Free Christian Church,—shops
and houses in abundance ; while if it be
reckoned to extend over the Golden Lion
Bridge as far as the Volunteer Inn, it now
contains no less than seven public-houses.
And all this in the last thirty years! There
is no necessity to go to Chicago for an instance of rapid development. New Swindon
is the Chicago of the western counties. This
Bridge Street, now so much used, was formerly
a mere track made by waggon wheels across
furrows, which crossed the canal at the Golden
Lion Bridge. That bridge, by the bye, is a
disgrace to the town. Where thirty years ago
stood trees, now stand lamp-posts! Instead of
rails and stakes there are now scaffolding-poles;
and what was once turf is now hard road.

This is what the railroad and factory have done for Swindon.

This factory is perhaps the largest in the West of England.[1]   Here are employed as

---

[1] In a paper by A. H. Mallan, on "The Great Western Railway Works at Swindon," we read :—

"In inspecting the works two points impress themselves on the mind :

"1. The economy of mechanical power, through duplication of work.

"2. The giant forces, invisible and unsuspected, literally beneath the feet, only requiring the touch of a handle to exert tremendous power in divers ways and methods.

"The wood-working department is the most captivating part of the whole works; partly on account of the resinous, turpentine smell, deliciously refreshing as compared with the oily atmosphere of the rest.

＊　　　＊　　　＊　　　＊　　　＊

"In the forges, an elaborate example of welding and building up is met with in the case of engine and truck wheels. These, in their earlier stages, consist of several sections, which are stamped out in dies under the steam hammer. One section forms a segment of the rim and outer part of the spoke; another, which is stamped in duplicate and sawn by a circular saw, gives the inner half of the spoke and segment of the centre. The two sections being then welded together, are ready to be framed for receiving the washers which form the boss. They are temporarily held together by an iron hoop, and after being brought to a white heat at the centre, are placed under the bossing hammer; a white hot washer is then placed on the centre, to be securely fixed by one mighty thump of the

many as seventeen hundred hands—an army
of workmen—drawn from the villages round
about. Here are made the engines used upon
the Great Western Railway. It is open to
visitors upon every Wednesday afternoon, and
is a sight well worth seeing. A person is in
attendance to show it. The place seems to
be built somewhat in the form of a parallelo-
gram. Seven tall chimneys belch forth vol-
umes of smoke. The first thing shown to
visitors is an engine room near the entrance.
Here are two beams of fifty horse-power working with a smooth, oily motion, almost without
noise. The yard beneath is, to a stranger, a

hammer; another washer is welded, while at white heat, by
a hydraulic press known as a veeing machine. The whole
operation presents a most picturesque appearance. The
men standing round the hammer, with one dazzling spot in
their midst, their outlines thrown into highest relief by
the strong glare from the neighbouring forges, pose themselves naturally, and produce an excellent Rembrandtesque
effect.

"Noise there is more or less everywhere; but the finest
effects of genuine ear-splitting clatter are met with in the
riveting shops. Hydraulic riveters do all the work within
their reach, giving just one noiseless 'squelch' with their
great crab-like callipers upon the red hot iron, and leaving
a neatly-shaped head where the long exposed end of the
rivet previously protruded."

vast incongruous museum of iron; iron in every possible shape and form, round and square, crooked and straight. Proteus himself never changed into the likeness of such things. The northern shops are devoted to noise, and the voice of the guide is inaudible. Here is a vast wilderness—an endless vista of forges glaring with blue flames, the men all standing by leaning upon their hammers, waiting until you pass, while far ahead sparks fly in showers from the tortured anvils high in the air, looking like minute meteors. This place is a temple of Vulcan. If the old motto *"Laborare est orare,"* "labour is prayer," is correct, here be sturdy worshippers of the fire-god. The first glimpse of the factory affords a view of sparks, sweat, and smoke. Smoke, sweat, and sparks is the last thing that is seen.

Passing between a row of fiery furnaces seven times heated, the visitors enter the rail-mill, where the rails are manufactured. This place is a perfect pandemonium. Vast boilers built up in brick close in every side, with the steam hissing like serpents in its efforts to escape. Enormous fly-wheels spin round and round at a velocity which renders the spokes invisible

Steam hammers shake the ground, where once
perhaps crouched the timid hare, and stun the
ear. These hammers are a miracle of human
manufacture. Though it is possible to strike a
blow which shall crush iron like earthenware,
to bring down a weight of tons, yet a skilful
workman can crack a hazel-nut without injuring
the kernel. Gazing upon these wonderful
hammers the visitor is suddenly scorched upon
one side, and turning, finds that a wheel-barrow
load of red-hot iron had been thrown down
beside him, upon which a jet of water plays,
fizzing off into steam. Springing aside he
scarcely escapes collision with a mass of red
hot metal wheeled along and placed beneath
the steam hammer, where it is thumped and
bumped flat. His feet now begin to feel the
heat of the iron flooring, which the thickest
leather cannot keep out. The workmen wear
shoes shod with broad headed iron nails from
heel to toe. Their legs are defended by
greaves—like an iron cricketing pad ; their
faces by a gauze metal mask. The clang, the
rattle, the roar are indescribable ; the confusion
seems to increase the longer it is looked upon.
Yonder, a glare almost too strong for the eyes

shows an open furnace door. Out comes a mass of white-hot metal, it is placed on a truck, and wheeled forward to the revolving rollers, and placed between them. Sparks spurt out like a fountain of fire—slowly it passes through, much thinned and lengthened by the process : which is repeated until at length it emerges in the form of a rail. Here come chips of iron —if such an expression might be used—all red hot, sliding along the iron floor to their destination. Look out for your toes! In the dark winter nights the glare from this place can be seen for miles around ; lighting up the clouds with a lurid glow like that from some vast conflagration. The shop known as the R Shop is the most interesting. Here iron is cut, and shaved as if it were wood. A vast hall filled with engines of all stages finishes the factory.

The factory and the place generally will always be connected with the name of Sir Daniel Gooch,[1] who was for so long a period

---

[1] No engines in the world have so long and so famous a history as the old engines of Sir Daniel Gooch. It is indeed surprising that a type decided upon so early as 1846 ("The North Briton") should be found capable of performing the duties of express engine in 1891, when the weight

intimately associated with it. A vast audience
in the hall of the Mechanics' Institute was held
in spell-bound silence scarce a twelvemonth
since, when that celebrated man gave a short
account of his career : how when but a youth
he had stood upon a bridge in Newcastle all
but despairing, when he chanced to observe a
motto cut upon it in large letters : "*Nil desper-
andum*"—" Never despair "—which from that
moment he adopted as his own. New Swindon
will never forget Sir Daniel Gooch, [1] whilst
the Mechanics' Institute affords the mechanic
a chance of becoming acquainted with literature, and the factory of earning a decent liveli-
hood.

Old Swindon has shared in the change
brought about by the enormous influx of population which followed the construction of the
Great Western Railway, But in Old Swindon—
a place dating from the Danish times—changes

of the trains is at least double that which they were designed to draw.

[1] Born 1816, died 1889. Became Chairman of the Great
Western Railway when its stock stood at 38½, until it rose
to 160.   Made a baronet for his services in connection with
the Atlantic Cable, 1866.

and improvements long preceded the very existence of the New Town. The Old Swindon
of to-day is very new in comparison with the
Swindon of seventy years ago; for then there
was but one Swindon. Immediately without the
town is a well-known field called the " Butts,"
probably the place where archery was practised
when the bow and arrow was the principal
weapon of the English army. This must have
been in use not less than two centuries ago,
perhaps more; for though in the reign of
Charles II. archery bands were still formed,
the bow and arrow do not seem to have been
used in the Civil War, except indeed, perhaps,
in the North of Scotland. (See Scott's novel,
Montrose, on that point.) The associations
then connected with this field belong to a
period coeval with that in which the Bell
Hotel, High Street, was built, which appears
from the date affixed to have been in 1581.
Queen Elizabeth then sat upon the throne of
England. The Spanish Armada had not yet
put forth to sea. Higher up the street, upon
the same side, there is a house now occupied
by Pakeman Brothers, which bears the date of
1631. Mr. Gillett's is dated 1741. Thirteen

years after this, or in 1754, a person by the
name of Robert Sadler was born in Swindon.[1]
He made himself in a certain sense notorious
by the publication of a work called *Wanley
Penson ; or, the Melancholy Man.*

Then, and for long after,[2] bull-baiting was no

---

[1] Sadler lived afterwards at Chippenham and at Malmesbury. His father, who was a glover and breeches maker,
was a member of the Moravian Brethren, and the novel
of *Wanley Penson* deals with the tenets of this sect. He
also wrote *The Discarded Spinster ; or, a Plea for the
Poor*, dealing with the effects of the introduction of ma-
chinery into the manufacture of cloth. He left two other
works in manuscript. The description of his personal appearance so closely resembles that of Richard Jefferies that
it is here quoted in full.

Britton says of Sadler : —

" He was a man of singular person, manners and abili-
ties. Had the same mind been well instructed and dis-
ciplined in early life, it might have become eminent in art,
in literature, or in science ; for it manifested, on many occasions, the rudiments and principles, as well as the union of
philosophy and poetry. . . . Like most sedentary,
studious persons, his whole frame was morbid, the muscles
relaxed and the nervous system deranged, his physical
powers were always weak and languid.

" In person, he was tall, thin, and apparently in a state of
consumption. The face was narrow and pale, the cheeks
collapsed, his general physiognomy that of an abstracted
and melancholy, but highly intellectual man."

[2] Probably until nearly 1812.

uncommon thing at Swindon. The sport was
carried on in the Square, and the stone post to
which the bull was tied was removed in the
memory of man; though it had not been used
for some time previously. Swindon once
boasted a market-house, just as it now boasts
a corn exchange; the difference being that,
whereas the modern building is a substantial
erection of stone, the place was supported upon
oaken pillars. It was pulled down in the year
1793. Close by stood the stocks and whip-
ping-post, which were taken down about the
same time.

Wood Street—that fashionable street, the
Strand of Swindon—was then known as Black-
smith Street. There were three blacksmiths'
forges in it, from which it was named, and the
noise and smoke from them, when in full
vigour, was something intolerable. Some enterprising persons actually erected a windmill
here, but the speculation was unsuccessful; it
was taken down, and three cottages built with
the materials, which three cottages stood where
now the King's Arms Inn offers shelter and
good cheer to travellers. Wood Street had in
the memory of man a very pleasant appear-

ance. Trees and shrubs grew in one spot;
and against the walls of the houses on the
northern side—that which receives the sunshine—were trained a number of vines. One
of these vines, which were remarkably strong
and vigorous, being protected by chains or
railings from injury to the stem, grew against
the wall of Messrs. Edwards & Suter, the iron-
mongers' shop; another against that of Mr.
Pimbury, and a third displayed its tempting
clusters of grapes upon the wall of an old
cottage which once stood upon the spot which
the post-office now occupies. Wood Street
has lost this pleasant appearance. At this date
there were so many things not to be found at
Swindon, that a modern might exclaim there
was nothing at all in it. Firstly, there was no
railroad, nor canal. There were no banks, and
if there were dissenters there were at least no
chapels. There were no newspapers, nor any
one to print them, nor booksellers to sell them
—not even so much as a stationer's shop,
which almost every village can now boast.
There was no druggist, nor patent medicine
dealer—perhaps little the worse for that—and
lastly there were no watchmakers. Those

large brazen-faced clocks, which can be found
in almost every farmhouse in the neighbourhood, never bear the imprint of a Swindon
maker.   Cricklade and Lyneham were famous
places for clocks.   At this date progress was
indeed slow.   In a course of twenty years five
new houses were built.   No living to be got
by house-building!   Contracts are things of
modern date.   They built houses very leisurely
in former times, but they had this advantage,
they were built well.

The railway had one effect at Swindon which
was immediately perceptible.   It knocked the
coaching business on the head.   Swindon had
been a stage between Cheltenham and South-
ampton.   The next was Marlborough, whither
a coach ran from the Goddard Arms daily.   It
was long driven by a man of the name of
Danvers, and was usually drawn by three pie-
bald horses.   The starting of this coach was
the event of the day in Swindon.   The windows were crowded by spectators—chiefly
ladies—whose curiosity seems to have been as
great then as now.   The old inhabitants maintain that Swindon, despite its increased population, has never seemed so gay as in the

coaching times. It was by no means unusual
for persons to walk out of town in the afternoon, meet the coach, and ride back in it.
There was another coach which went to Hungerford, *en route* for London, a journey which
then occupied a whole day, from six in the
morning till six at night, and cost a guinea in
matter of fare.

In those times the petty sessions were conducted in a small room at the Goddard Arms
Inn, with closed doors, only a few favoured
individuals being allowed entrance. It was
remarked that offences against the game laws
were usually visited by severe penalties. There
was no police station—the police being represented by a single constable. At night a
watchman perambulated the streets, staff in
hand, who at intervals cried the hours, adding
the state of the weather. Prisoners were confined in a place most appropriately called the
Black Hole, which was at the top of Newport
Street, then known as Bull Street, on the spot
now occupied by the engine house. It was a
small, damp, and dirty dungeon, half under
ground; lighted by a hole in the door crossed
with iron bars, through which those that were

within might converse with those without, or
suck in beer by the aid of a tobacco pipe.   For
their meals they were conducted to the Bull
Inn, thus affording them a capital chance of a
rescue.   This place was a disgrace to the town.
The credit of its removal must in a great
measure be given to Mr. C. A. Wheeler.

Another effect of the railway on Old Swindon was the building of houses in Prospect
Place and the New Road.   Swindon, like other
places which are progressing, shows a tendency
to extend itself westward ; scarcely a house
being added upon the eastern side.   The
Sands has become a fashionable promenade.
Persons formerly had to go to Marlborough if
they wished to go "shopping"; at present they
come to Swindon.   Swindon has, in short,
become the capital of North Wilts.

Christ Church is a landmark for miles
around.   It was consecrated upon Friday, the
7th of November, 1852, by the Lord Bishop of
Llandaff; the sermon upon the occasion being
preached by the Rev. Giles Daubeney.   The
length of the structure is 130 feet ; the breadth,
exclusive of the transepts, nave, and chancel,
50 feet ; and the tower, with the spire, rises

165 feet. The great stained-glass window was
uncovered on the 7th November, 1855. It
consists of five lancet divisions. The small
quatrefoils contain the arms of Grooby and
Vilett; the larger have three illustrations taken
from the Old Testament—the offering for the
cleansing of a leper, the consecration of one
bird and the flight of another; the brazen ser-
pent; and the offering of the first-fruits of the
harvest. The five divisions are separated into
three horizontal compartments, containing five
designs from the Bible—the Parable of the
Sower; the Pearl of Great Price; the Net cast
into the Sea; the Pharisee and the Publican;
the Good Shepherd; the Prodigal Son; and
the Good Samaritan. The inscription at the
foot states that the window was erected " to the
honour and glory of God, and in memory of
the Rev. Jas. Grooby, many years vicar of the
parish, by his widow, Catherine Mary Grooby,
and also to the memory of her brother, Lieut.-
Col. Vilett." It was made at Newcastle-on-
Tyne, in the manufactory of Mr. Wailes, and
was pronounced by him the best he had done,
or probably should do. No expense was
spared upon the window—*carte blanche* being

given—and it is considered by the admirers of such productions as most beautiful.

Swindon has now [1867] an increasing population of 8,000.[1] It is lighted by gas, and has many public buildings, of all of which full descriptions have appeared in the *North Wilts Herald*. Its situation is dry and healthy. It stands perhaps upon the highest spot above the sea in the midland western counties; the neighbourhood being the watershed of three rivers. A spring, passing through Brudhill, and joined by the water from another which rises almost beneath the family mansion of the Goddards, runs down to near the canal, where, falling into a brook coming from Chiseldon, through Coate, it proceeds through Rawborough and Coleshill to join the Thames or Isis River near Inglesham. That spring, which rises near to the Goddard mansion, formerly supplied a large pond close to the churchyard, which had a very pleasant appearance, and supplied large numbers with good water. Horses could be watered here. The same

[1] The present population (1896) is about 36,000, an increase in thirty years which has been exceeded by few English towns.

spring drove a water-wheel immediately beneath. The old mill has been down some years, but the pond has been only lately filled up. A pump stands there now, and a plot of rhododendrons covers the space once occupied by water. A second spring, rising at Wroughton, runs through Blagrove and Rodbourne Cheney, on to Cricklade, where it also falls into the Thames. A third spring rises between Lower Upham and Draycott Foliatt, close to the Marlborough Road, runs through Ogbourne, and joins the Kennet at Mildenhall, near Marlborough. A fourth rises at Hackpen, passes by Abury, and is the mainspring of the Kennet. Finally, a fifth rises at Solthrop, runs through Wootton Bassett, and at length falls into the Avon. Hence it will be seen that three rivers—the Thames, Kennet, and Avon—receive supplies either from Swindon itself,[1] or the immediate neighbourhood.

[1] "Thus the waters of Wiltshire find their way from the heart of the county respectively to the Atlantic, the English Channel, and the German Ocean."—*R. N. Worth.*

CHAPTER IV

UPPER UPHAM

"Old John of Gaunt—time-honoured Lancaster."
—*Shakespeare.*

UPPER UPHAM lies about seven miles from Swindon in an easterly direction. It simply consists of a mansion and an adjoining cottage or two, which stands upon the summit of a ridge of downs immediately behind Liddington Castle—that conspicuous and well-known landmark to all the neighbourhood round about. It is so named to distinguish it from Lower Upham — a farmhouse standing beneath in the vale. Here is a strange avenue of sycamore trees, through which runs the way from Marlborough road to Upper Upham. After leaving Lower Upham the ground im-

mediately commences to ascend. On the left
hand there is a conspicuous "tump" or
"hump," in the language of the locality, that
is, a mound covered with turf, which has been
considered a tumulus, but is not sufficiently
distinct to be so called without further and
internal examination. Upon the top of the
first ridge of downs, overlooking Lower
Upham and the plain of Chiseldon, there is a
piece of arable land. Here, some time since,
the plough turned up some portions of mosaic-
work in a very perfect state of preservation,
supposed to have once formed the floor of a
Roman villa, or some other structure of the
Roman period. This mosaic was formerly in
the possession of the present occupier of Upper
Upham farm, Mr. Frampton, a courteous
gentleman, to whose untiring exertion and
intelligent investigations the present author
owes most of the facts he is here enabled
to lay before the reader. It is much to
be regretted that this mosaic has been
mislaid, probably through the carelessness of
servants, and it is still more to be regretted
that no excavations have been made upon the
site of the discovery, excavations which might

be expected to yield much interesting matter calculated to throw light upon the manners of the Romans during their long stay in Britain. Upper Upham, though a mansion of great extent and height, and though placed upon the summit of a ridge of the downs, is yet so concealed by trees that it is only when standing immediately before it that anything of a view can be obtained. The gabled roof, mullioned windows, and gigantic porch at once convey an impression of antiquity, which is borne out upon investigation. The porch is sufficiently high to enable a person on horseback to sit beneath it as a sentinel, like the Horse Guards at Whitehall. Perhaps in ancient days the door was of a similar height to allow of a horseman riding into the hall of the mansion— an occurrence by no means uncommon if tradition and ballads are worthy of credence. The champion rides into Westminster Hall at the coronation dinner even in the present age, and in the old metrical romance of King Estmere (supposed to have been written late in the fifteenth century, perhaps about 1491), there is a plain allusion to such a custom. King Estmere, in order to obtain entrance to

his lady love, who is sitting at her marriage-
feast beside the paynim King of Spain—by
compulsion be it understood—disguises himself
as a minstrel, and, in company with his brother,
"Adler Yonge," who carries his harp, rides up
to the hall gate. The porter intimates that he
does not recognize them.

> "Then they pulled out a ryng of gold
>   Layd itt on the porter's arme :
> 'And ever we will thee, proud porter,
>   Thou wilt saye us no harme.'
> Sore he looked on Kyng Estmere
>   And sore he handled the ryng,
> Then opened to them the fayre hall yates,
>   He lett for no kind of thyng.

> "Kyng Estmere he stabled his steede
>   Soe fayre att the hall borde
> The frothe that came from his brydle bitte
>   Light on King Bremor's beard.
> Saies, 'Stable thou steede thou proud harper,
>   Goe, stable him in the stalle ;
> Itt doth not beseeme a proud harper,
>   To stable him in a Kyng's halle.' "

A fight ensues, in which King Estmere and
"Adler Yonge" vanquish the whole paynim
host, by help of "grammarye," that is magic,
and finally convey the bride home.

Now upon the arch of the porch is the following inscription :—

```
R.G.
1559
E.G.
```

which date is not much more than a century after the date of the above ballad. These initials are those of the Goddards of Cliffe, or Cleeve, who at that time owned the Upper Upham estate. This antique porch being in a very faulty state, and threatening destruction, instead of affording shelter, to those who passed beneath, was some time since repaired, but without altering its original appearance. High over the porch hangs a bell, used for divers purposes—it was cast in the neighbouring village of Aldbourne. The mansion is built of flint and stone, the first being a material easily obtainable upon these downs, whence are taken hundreds of cart-loads in the course of a year for repairing the adjacent highways. The porch before mentioned gives entrance to what was originally one vast hall, extending the whole length of the building. At present this enormous apartment is partitioned off into two —a sitting-room and a drawing-room—another portion of it forms a passage ; and a fourth is still used for the purposes for which a modern hall is required. This must have been a magnificent apartment in times gone by. Hundreds of retainers might have sat at table in the body of the hall, looked down upon by "my lord," sitting on the daïs, or raised portion ; which at this day forms a drawing-room whose floor is still elevated a step or two above that of the other apartments. When the size of this immense apartment is thoroughly understood and conceived, it is impossible not to marvel at the vastness of the ideas of our ancestors. Here, perched upon a wild range of down, utterly unseen, and unheard of by the traveller, far distant from any other habitation, is a mansion which might compete, perhaps, with any in North Wilts, for the original extent of its apartments, and most certainly in the traditions and associations connected with them. At the present date the neighbourhood seems deserted, but then it must have been possible to collect hundreds together, since guests to fill the im-

mense hall must certainly have required to be
numbered by the hundred.

The present sitting-room contains two objects
of especial interest. The first is a carved
mantelpiece, of great width, height, and antiquity ; there are few things here that are not
at the same time ancient and immense. It
takes a tall man to reach anything off this
mantelpiece. But above it is an attraction to
the antiquary. It is a large square tablet—if
such an expression may be used—containing a
carved coat-of-arms. The centre-piece is much
defaced ; one of the supporters is completely
gone, and the other so much mutilated that it
seems impossible to pronounce it either a griffin
or an unicorn ; probably it is the latter. A ducal
crown projects above, with what appear enormous oak leaves. Beneath is a scroll carved at
full length with the inscription : " Dieu et mon
droit." [1] The whole is surrounded by a carved
border. This is considered to be the coat-of-

---

[1] Mr. Morris says : " It would seem from this that there
is nothing more than tradition for it that Upper Upham
was ever a royal hunting seat. And it must be further
noticed that the tradition, as handed down by John Britton
and the Rev. J. Seagram, does not exactly tally, the former

arms of Lancaster. When John of Gaunt, the
son of King Edward the Third, was created
Duke of Lancaster by his father, at the ceremony of investure he was not only girded by
the King with a sword, but a cap of fur under-
neath a coronet of gold set with jewels was
placed upon his head. He seems to have been
the first who was thus, as it were, crowned.
Here on this coat-of-arms may still be seen
the representation of this ducal crown, which
exactly answers the description given of the
original. These are the arms[1] of the celebrated
John of Gaunt, "time-honoured Lancaster."

referring to the place as being the hunting seat of King
John, who reigned from 1189 to 1199, and the latter to
John of Gaunt, who died 1398. Of course, it may be that
both King John and John of Gaunt made use of Upper
Upham as a hunting seat. And this would seem to be
very probable. King John's connection with Marlborough,
the almost adjoining parish, is well authenticated."

Mr. Waylen, in his *History of Marlborough*, says : " John's
connection with Marlborough is still further testified by the
fact that he selected it as the scene of his marriage with the
heiress of the Earl of Gloucester, which took place in con-
formity with Richard's wishes, and in all probability with the
sanction of his presence, 29th August, 1189."

[1] The arms of John of Gaunt, Duke of Lancaster, were :
"France and England quarterly, with a label of three
points, ermine, with the garter."

The motto is that of the monarchs of England :
" God and my right."

At the back of the hall are the offices and
staircase. The staircase is of carved oak in
good preservation, and occupies much room.
Immediately over the hall is a chamber known
as the " banqueting room." This, too, is on
the same scale. It is at least thirty feet in
length, and of corresponding breadth and
height. Here is another carved mantelpiece,
considered to be of Jacobean times. It is in
excellent preservation. The supporters on
either hand are carved figures. What indescribable scenes of revelry this chamber in
all probability witnessed in the days of long
ago! Whilst the rude retainers quaffed, and
roared forth their drinking songs in the
spacious hall beneath, those of more noble
birth feasted here. Every window—and there
were three to this banqueting room, though
now but one—glared forth upon the night with
the light of the flames in the fireplace, or the
flaring torches. Two cart-loads of wood, says
tradition, was the allowance of yonder yawning
chimney-place from sunset to sunrise. Here
the strangely-dressed courtiers of Queen Eliza-

beth's time feasted and drank, and discussed
court scandal. There is a tradition that Queen
Elizabeth herself once spent a night or two in
this old mansion during one of her progresses.
Francis Rutland, a courtier who died during a
progress, lies buried in Chiseldon Church, not
much over two miles distant. Here the
cavaliers of King Charles's days roared out their
tipsy loyalty, and swore deep oaths of deadly
vengeance against " Old Noll," whose soldiers,
says tradition, destroyed as far as they were
able the carved coat-of-arms in the hall beneath.
It bore the royal motto—that was enough—
down with it! Musket butt, or pike-end—
destroy the idol Baal! Such was the fierce
unreasoning hatred of the Parliamentarian
soldiers to everything which symbolized
monarchy. King Charles himself may have
caught a hurried glance at these ancient walls,
for he was often in the neighbourhood, and
once or twice passed very near, as will be
presently shown. The men of times long
before these, men of plate-armour, two-handed
swords and battle-axes, may have taken refreshment here for aught that is distinctly
known to the contrary. That old oaken stair-

case may have felt the iron tread of mailed men, and re-echoed to the clank of their long swords and jingling spurs. These vast halls carry back the mind to a period of English history long gone by—far back to the days of steel. These are the days of steam.

The very elevated situation upon which the mansion is built may be easily realized when it is stated that, with the aid of a good telescope, Windsor can be seen upon the one hand, and Brecon, in Wales, on the other. This is, of course, from the upper storeys.

The mansion, or the estate at least, was in ancient days one of those in the possession of John of Gaunt, the most remarkable man of his age. His relation to royal personages would have been sufficient to have made his name in a certain sense famous, he being the son of a king, the brother of a king, and the uncle of a king. But it was as a military commander that John of Gaunt chiefly shone.[1] Shakespeare has immortalised his name in the historical drama of Richard II. He probably held the

---

[1] Historians may be allowed to differ from Jefferies' opinion in this as in other matters noted throughout these pages.

Upper Upham estate by some form of feudal tenure.

Now it is very evident that the present mansion of Upper Upham does not date from that remote period. There is a very marked alteration in the face of the country immediately upon leaving Upper Upham. Here, perhaps, upon these wild and, to a great extent, unenclosed downs, may be seen the nearest approach to the ancient state of Britain—wide, open campaign country, with clumps of trees and forest glades interspersed, once the resort and favourite haunt of deer. Beneath, in the vale, the country is of an entirely different description. There it is rich meadow land, looking, from the summit of the downs, like one extensive wood, from the numberless trees growing in the thick hedges, together with the interspersed copses. Here is ridge after ridge of down, with an occasional copse, a fir plantation, clumps of trees, wild glades, and deep secluded vales, all open and unenclosed, a rare hunting country. Moreover, the down upon the south of Upham is to this day known as [1]Ald-

[1] Also spelt in old maps, Auburn, Albourn, and Aldbourn.

bourne Chace. Chace is a well-known word meaning wood. Some maps call it the Royal Chace; but the name most commonly used for the last two centuries has been Aldbourne Chace. There is a wood there to this day, and it is a favourite meet for hounds—for such a length of time do customs exist in England. This place, where centuries ago the wild deer ran free, except when the hounds were upon their track, is to this day famous for hunting. Hence it seems a reasonable conclusion that Upper Upham was a hunting-lodge; much such another mansion as that which is familiar to the readers of Sir Walter Scott's *Woodstock*. The building itself bears out this conjecture. So vast a hall could never have been needed by a country gentleman, or simple lord of the manor, nor are the other portions of the mansion in proportion to it. It is very evident that it was only used on certain occasions when the hunt had run this way. But then comes the immediate question—to what forest was this a hunting lodge? Some say Windsor, but the great distance from that place seems to offer an almost insuperable objection. Others prefer Savernake, but that forest does not appear to have extended in this direction. There remains Braden Forest, which was formerly of enormous extent, and which even at the present day is a large wood. Braden Forest has this recommendation—it was held by the Dukes of Lancaster by some form of tenure from the Crown, and here at Upper Upham may still be seen the Lancastrian coat of arms. The distance is much less than Windsor. Braden Wood lies immediately below Purton, a little over twelve miles distant, Burderop Wood lies three miles distant, almost in a direct line. At Burderop there were deer no great time ago. Horns are still preserved which were shed by the deer of Burderop. At any rate there can be but little doubt that Upper Upham was a hunting lodge, to whatever forest it may have been attached.

The present mansion is certainly a more modern erection than that which belonged to John of Gaunt in the fourteenth century, though some of the material with which it is constructed may have come from the more ancient erection. In the wall of the garden may be seen a stone carved with ovals, evidently never intended for its present position.

Similar stones are built into the adjoining
stable. One of them has the letter E cut upon
it, while the beams of the stable are of black
oak, and carved ; nor does the stable appear to
have been ever used for any other purpose
than that to which it is put at present. These
stones and beams may have formed part of an
ancient building, the site of which was somewhat south of the present mansion. Here, on
the edge of the hill, may be seen great irregularities and unevenness in the ground. This
field still goes by the name of the Rookery,
though now there is scarcely a tree to be seen
in it, and the position of the present rookery
is immediately behind the modern mansion.
Moreover, on the very edge of the hill, in the
south-eastern corner of the field, there may still
be seen a hollow in the ground, of a circular
shape, which has four well-marked entrances,
and three tiers, or steps, like a miniature am-
phitheatre. It is, in short, a cockpit. All this
would seem to mark the site of an ancient
building, and more decided testimony is yet
forthcoming. One old lady, who has now been
dead many years, but who lived to be ninety,
and whose memory might, therefore, commence

a full century since, used to aver that in her
youth there still remained the visible ruins of a
building, two or three feet high, upon or near
those places now rendered remarkable by the
unevenness of the ground. There were also
deep caverns underground—vaults, or cellars—
in which smugglers were accustomed to con-
ceal their goods after a run upon the south
coast. That there are caverns and hollow
places underground here and near about is a
known fact. It is remarkable that at the
present day all the water used for drinking
purposes here is brought from the village of
Shap, at some very considerable distance,
where there is a deep well, with a wheel made
to revolve by a pony.[1] Our ancestors were
not usually accustomed to place their habitations where there was no water to be got.
They always had to face the risk of a siege.
It is probable that there was a well here somewhere, though it is now choked and the site
unknown. There is a tradition that an attempt
was once made to get water here by sinking a
well, which attempt, after having been carried
to a depth of three cart lines, or 120 feet, was

[1] *Cf.* the well at Carisbrooke Castle.

H

abandoned, and the excavation walled over. Some while afterwards a carter was driving a loaded wagon over the spot, utterly ignorant of what was beneath, when he was alarmed by a horrible noise, felt the ground tremble, dropped his whip, and ran for his life. Looking behind him, he found that his team and wagon had disappeared down a chasm in the earth—the old lost well. Later, whilst making a hole with an iron bar in the present yard, the bar suddenly sank through, and a hazel rod of great length having been procured, was let down without reaching the bottom. In the vale beneath the ground still known as the Rookery, tradition states that there was once a magnificent row of oaks extending to the village of Aldbourne, and the place to this day is known as Fair-Oak Vale.

Near the present mansion, in a field known as the Longfield, on the edge of the hill over-looking Aldbourne Warren, there are some more unmistakable traces of ancient habitations. The ground is very uneven, mounds running across it in all directions, though seeming chiefly to enclose parallelograms. On one spot there grows a large quantity of daffodils, so

firmly rooted that it has been found impossible
to eradicate them. They cover a considerable
space of ground, and can always be discovered
on account of the sheep refusing to eat the
leaves, and treading them under foot. This
was probably a garden. There does not
appear to have been any tradition concerning
this place, whence it may be concluded that if
habitations were to be found here it was at a
time long previous to the erection of those
whose ruins were seen by the old lady who has
been mentioned.

Hence there are three different periods, as it
were, represented at Upper Upham.[1] The pre-

[1] Mr. Morris writes, in *Swindon Fifty Years Ago* : "This,
then, is what I would suggest as the probable history of
Upper Upham, and the interesting old mansion there, and
it will be allowed that the suggestion has the advantage of
admitting the possibility of all the things we have heard
about the place. That there was a mansion or hunting
seat which belonged to either King John or John of Gaunt,
and possibly to both; that this house fell into ruins; that
in 1541 John Goddard, of Aldbourne, acquired the lands
at Upper Upham on which the ruins were, along with lands
in Wanborough, Wiclescote, and Wroughton, which lands
had previously belonged to Lacock Abbey, through a grant
from the Crown; and that John Goddard's successor to the
property, Richard Goddard, built the present house, not
far from where the old royal hunting seat had stood, and

sent mansion carries the mind back three centuries; the ruins of the Rookery to a time that
survives only in tradition; the traces in the
Longfield to a period of which nothing is
known, and but little conjectured.

Coins of almost all periods of English history have been found upon the Upper Upham
estate, and are in the possession of the present
occupier. The Britons are represented by a
gold coin, whose intrinsic value—that is, as
simply a piece of gold—is estimated at 13s. 6d.
It is a coin of a very early period, being
without inscription, and may probably have
been made before Christ. It is decidedly con-
cave on one side, and convex on the other.
The device is in excellent preservation, and
consists of the rude figure of a horse—much
like a miniature representation of the sculp-

---

using therefore in the building such stones and material as
was available from the ruins; and that probably, some
thirty years afterwards, the entrance porch not satisfying
the critical eye of Sir Christopher Wren, was altered as it
now stands in accordance with his designs. I am unable
to say how long the property remained in the Goddard
family after 1599, but I believe I am correct in saying it
was repurchased some years ago by the present representa-
tive of the family, Mr. A. L. Goddard."

tured horse on the down at Woolston—and
two chariot wheels, one above and the other
beneath the horse. A few uncertain flourishes
are scattered about. These coins are con
sidered to be rude imitations of the " Philips,"
issued by the Macedonian monarchs, long before Christ, and which went all over Europe.
These Philips had on one side Apollo driving
a chariot. British coins have been found
which illustrate the gradual decline of the
imitation from the artistic excellence of the
original to the rudeness of conception which
characterizes this coin discovered at Upper
Upham. It may be a coin of the Belgæ, mentioned by Richard of Cirencester as a tribe
holding a large part of Wiltshire, who were
foreigners arriving in Britain from Gaul before
the advent of Cæsar.

Two Roman copper coins, with illegible inscriptions, a gold crown of Henry the Eighth,
one with a large P with two cross-bars, others
marked with a dragon, a medal of Elizabeth
with an inscription stating that she was a rose
without a thorn, and several others of later
date, have been found here, and are preserved
together with a very fine barbed arrowhead.

Another Roman relic is also carefully kept. It
is a brass ornament of a trumpet with an inscription in very primitively formed letters—
Gaudeamus—that is, " Let us rejoice."

The village of Aldbourne (pronounced Awborne) lies at a short distance from Upper
Upham. "Sweet Auburn! loveliest village of
the plain," is the opening line of Goldsmith's
"Deserted Village." Aldbourne lies in a plain,
and it has been thought that this is the spot
alluded to by the poet,[1] who allows that the
misery he sings of only existed in his imagination. Aldbourne is a very ancient place. John
of Gaunt gave a charter to Aldbourne, in which
he gave eighty acres to the poor of the parish,
which exists to this day in much the same state
as it may be supposed to have been then—wild
and uncultivated. Aldbourne was once famous

---

[1] This is only a fancy. Auburn was a mere name,
which may have referred to Lissoy, Co. Westmeath, but in
all probability referred to a place which only existed in the
poet's imagination. Macaulay says: "The village, in its
happy days, is a true English village; the village in its
decay is an Irish village. The felicity and the misery
which Goldsmith has brought together belong to two
different countries, and to two different stages in the progress of society." There is nothing in this locality to lend
colour to Jefferies' theory.

for its bell foundry; but this is a thing of the past. A fine set of bells cast here is in the church tower. Old Swindon chime is said to have been cast at Aldbourne. Aldbourne Warren was once a famous place for rabbits. It was let out and rented like a farm. In winter, in frosty weather, it was often found necessary to take a wagon load of hay out, which the rabbits would follow by the thousand, like a flock of sheep, and no sooner was it flung down than it was devoured. Aldbourne rabbits were in great favour in the London markets, and rabbits are said to be still sold there under that name, though perhaps in reality no rabbit has been sent there in the present century from Aldbourne.

The following extract from Lord Clarendon's history of the Rebellion relates to Aldbourne Chace :—

" So that the Earl of Essex was march'd with his whole army and train from Tewkesbury, four-and-twenty hours before the King heard which way he was gone; for he took advantage of a dark night, and having sure Guides, reached Ciciter before the breaking of the day ; where he found two regiments of the

King's horse quartered securely; all which, by
the negligence of the officers (a common and
fatal crime throughout the War, on the King's
part), he surprised, to the number of above
three hundred; and, which was of much
greater value, he found there a great quantity
of provisions, prepared by the King's commis-
saries for the army before Gloster, and which
they neglected to remove after the siege was
raised, and so most sottishly left it for the relief
of the enemy, far more apprehensive of hunger
than of the sword; and indeed this wonderful
supply strangely exalted their spirits, as sent
by the special care and extraordinary hand of
Providence, even when they were ready to
faint.

"From hence the Earl, having no farther
apprehension of the King's horse, which he
had no mind to encounter upon the open cam-
pania, and being at the least twenty miles
before him, by easy marches, that his sick and
wearied soldiers might overtake him, moved,
through that deep and enclosed country of
North Wiltshire, his direct way to London.
As soon as the King had sure notice which
way the enemy was gone, he endeavoured by

expedition and diligence to recover the advantage which the supine negligence of those he
had trusted had robbed him of; and himself,
with matchless industry, taking care to lead up
the foot, prince Rupert with near five thousand
, horse, march'd day and night over the hills to
get between London and the enemy, before
they should be able to get out of those enclosed deep countries, in which they were
engaged between narrow lanes, and to enter-
tain them with skirmishes till the whole army
should come up. This design, pursued and
executed with indefatigable pains, succeeded to
his wish; for when the van of the enemy's
army had almost marched over Awborne
Chase, intending that night to have reach'd
Newbury, prince Rupert, besides their fear or
expectation, appear'd with a strong body of
horse so near them, that before they could put
themselves in order to receive him, he charged
their rear, and routed them with good execution; and though the enemy performed the
parts of good men, and applied themselves
more dexterously to the relief of each other
than on so sudden and unlook'd for an occasion was expected, yet, with some difficulty and

the loss of many men, they were glad to shorten their journey, and, the night coming on, took up their quarters at Hungerford.

"In this conflict, which was very sharp for an hour or two, many fell of the enemy, and of the King's party none of name but the marquis of Vieu Ville, a gallant gentleman of the French nation, who had attended the Queen out of Holland, and put himself as a volunteer upon this action into the lord Jermin's regiment. There were hurt many officers, and among those the lord Jermin received a shot in his arm with a pistol, owing the preservation of his life from other shots to the excellent temper of his armour; and the lord Digby, a strange hurt in the face, a pistol being discharged at so near a distance upon him that the powder fetch'd much blood from his face, and for the present blinded him without further mischieve; by which it was concluded that the bullet had dropped out before the pistol was discharged. And it may be reckoned amongst one of those escapes, of which that gallant person hath passed a greater number in the course of his life than any man I know."

This skirmish in "Awborne Chace" so delayed
the Earl of Essex that the King was enabled
to come up, when ensued the battle of Newbury.[1] A memento of those bloody times was
picked up in Aldbourne Chace, not long since,
in the shape of a cannon ball, thought to weigh
about 8 lbs. A boy more lately made a very
fortunate discovery in the same Chace. He
saw something glitter upon the ground, picked
it up, and found it was a coin, which he supposed was a very old shilling. On further
investigation he discovered nearly two hundred
similar coins, and carried them home in a sack.
These coins are said to be of the reign of King
Charles ; hence they were probably hidden in
the Chace about the time of the Civil Wars.

[1] September 20th, 1643.

CHAPTER V

THE direct road to London from Swindon passes through Coate. Shortly after leaving that village, there may be seen at a little distance upon the left hand a long, low-roofed, ancient slated farm-building, known as Liddington Wick. It is now in the occupation of Mr. Reeves,[1] and is conspicuous for a great way, on account of a magnificent yew growing immediately before the house. Tradition states that Liddington Wick was once a Roman Catholic chapel or oratory, though to what monastery or nunnery it belonged is not said. It is evidently an ancient building, from the thickness of the walls, and that it was not originally destined for the purpose to which it is applied may be inferred from the fact that in

[1] Its present occupant is Mr. J. Smith.

the memory of man the front door resembled that of a church—heavy, and studded with nails. Moreover, the drawing-room contains a carved ceiling, cut in plaster of Paris or some similar material, which is said to be unique of its kind, and is of considerable antiquity. This ceiling was originally picked out in blue and gold, but is now a plain white. The pattern is that which is known in embroidery as the wheel. Liddington Wick is interesting, since it appears to be almost the only remaining vestige of Roman Catholic times in this neighbourhood. One version of the tradition makes it a nunnery. The fine yew immediately before the door gives it still a sombre appearance, suitable for a house used for religious purposes. This tree may date from the days of the nuns. It is evidently some centuries old. Before the mansion there is a field known as the home field. Through it the footpath to Lower Wanborough passes. Here there are unmistakable traces of ancient habitations, the ground being full of irregularities. While digging drains here coins were found, stated to be Roman. Liddington Wick is a place of great antiquity, and has been inhabited from time immemorial. A field near by here affords a curious fact to the lovers of natural history. It is covered with what appears at first sight simply small turfy and thymy hillocks of earth, but which turn out upon investigation to be ant-hills, placed so close together that it is possible by springing from one to the other to pass from one side of the ground to the other without setting foot on the level earth. These hillocks represent the industry of millions—countless myriads—of ants, continued, no doubt, for years, since the fields seem to have presented this appearance from time immemorial.

Liddington Wick is the outlying habitation of the ancient village of Liddington. Liddington is a well-known place. It has figured in novels ere now. A Mrs. May, the wife of a former rector of Liddington, combined the legends of Liddington into a tale of fiction some twenty years ago, and issued it to the public under the title of *The Abbess of Shaftesbury*, which work made a great noise in the neighbourhood at the date of its publication, but has now become rare. The plot circles round Liddington Manor-house. This mansion lies at the extremity—the mouth—of a narrow,

winding vale, sheltered from the north-easterly
winds by the downs, and has a beautiful view
of the vale beneath from the western windows.
A spring rising near forms some large ponds,
which give the place the appearance of being
surrounded with water, while a rookery and an
'ancient water-wheel add to the old English look
of the place. It is certainly the most romantic-
ally-situated mansion in the neighbourhood.
The many-gabled roofs and mullioned windows
proclaim its antiquity. It has been described
as Elizabethan, and such may be the style of
the building, but the inscription upon the
chimney-top is A. V. 1670. C. V., at which date
Charles II. was upon the English throne.
Here are supposed to take place the main
incidents in *The Abbess of Shaftesbury*, which
also contains allusions to John of Gaunt and
his mansion of Upper Upham. Liddington
Manor-house was well known to all the neighbourhood as the residence of the venerable Mr.
Brind. A carved mantelpiece here is said to
be of great age.

Liddington Church contains two tombs
which have caused much discussion in antiquarian circles. They are side by side, placed

near the present vestry-room, and are in memory of some departed dignitaries of the church, as is evident from the foliated crosses. There is neither inscription nor date. Tradition says they are the tombs of the Abbot and Abbess of the suppressed Abbey of Shaftesbury. Liddington, then, in all probability, once belonged to that ancient monastery. Liddington Wick may have had some connection with it also. Liddington Church is a prebendal church.

High above the village towers Liddington Hill, well known to dwellers in the locality, and conspicuous to all from the Folly, or group of trees at one end, and the well-marked "castle," or entrenchment, at the other. Liddington Camp is usually considered as Roman, but it may nevertheless have afforded defence to both Briton and Roman, Saxon and Dane. It is of great extent, and somewhat of a square form—probably the largest in North Wilts. Each side may measure two hundred yards. This camp was placed upon a very commanding spot. The view from here is magnificent. Flint-digging has been carried on within the entrenchment, and resulted in the discovery of

numerous coins, said to be Roman, spear-heads
and arrow-heads, together with pieces of rusty
iron, now of no particular form, but supposed
to be broken sword-blades. Here also was
found a kind of bodkin with a square head,
engraved with characters. Liddington Camp
consists of only one fosse, which is, however,
of great depth. It is very evident that this
place was never thrown up by a passing army
for a night's defence—it is too large and substantial. It was probably a station, and well
garrisoned. The Ridge Way, an ancient
British road, runs at the foot of the hill; and
the Ickleton Way passes through Badbury and
Chisledon almost immediately beneath. A
memento of battle-fields, fought in days long
after those of spear and arrow-head, is said to
have been picked up upon this hill in the shape
of a cannon ball. It was probably sent upon
its errand of destruction in the times of the
Civil War.

The road to Faringdon branches off from the
London road at Liddington, and passes through
Wanborough. Wanborough is a place of great
antiquity, and played a distinguished part in
the early history of England. " A.D. 592,"

writes Ethelwerd,[1] "there was a great slaughter on both sides, at a place called Wodnesbyrg, so that Ceawlin was put to flight, and died at the end of one more year." Ceawlin was a Saxon king of Wessex. He it was who, in conjunction with Cenric, another Saxon chief, routed a British army near Barbury. His life seems to have been spent in one continued round of fighting, in which he was generally successful, until this fatal battle of Wanborough. Fuller accounts state that he had contrived to make himself obnoxious both to the Britons and Saxons, who joined their forces and defeated him. This was over twelve centuries ago. The same chronicler states that "A.D. 715 Ina and Ceolred (Ceolric?) fought against those who opposed them in arms at Wothnesbeorghge,"[2] that is, Wanborough.[3] Wan-

---

[1] Ethelwerd dedicated his work to, and wrote it for the use of his relation, Matilda, daughter of Otho the Great, Emperor of Germany, by his first Empress Editha, who is mentioned in the Saxon Chron., A.D. 925. His chronicle is called, "The Chronicle of Fabius Ethelwerd, from the beginning of the world to the year of our Lord 975.'

[2] Wodnesburie = Wodensburgh (?).

[3] "Dr. Guest remarked that the great highways of Wessex all converge on Wanborough."— *Worth.*

borough has, then, witnessed at least two severe contests. Somewhat more than a mile from Lower Wanborough, near Stratton St. Margaret, is a place known as Wanborough Nythe. This may have been once a Roman station, the site of which was upon Covenham Farm, near to the edge of the Nythe brook. Numerous remnants of the Roman occupation have been found here—chiefly coins.[1] It is recorded that in the year 1689 as many as sixteen hundred or two thousand coins were discovered here in a single vessel. They were no doubt of various descriptions, but it is stated that they were Roman, and none of a later date than Commodus. Commodus became Emperor of the Roman Empire about 180 A.D. An ancient Roman road runs close by, coming from the direction of Wanborough, and going towards Cricklade and Cirencester. It is remarkably straight. The word Nythe is thought to be a corruption of the Latin Nidus, which might perhaps mean home, or station, an inhabited spot.

In Domesday Book Wanborough is written Wembergh. It was held by the Bishop of

[1] And pottery.

Winchester for the support of the minster. In
the days of Henry II., who reigned from 1154
to 1189, it belonged to William Longespee,
then Earl of Sarum, or Salisbury. The brother
of this earl was, in the thirteenth year of Henry
III., Justiciary of Ireland. Wanborough became his by gift from the Earl of Sarum, in
the year 1245, on the condition that it was
to be held under Longespee's descendants.
Stephen, Justiciary of Ireland, got, in 1252, a
grant enabling him to hold a market and fair
at Wanborough. He died in 1260. Wanborough then fell to his widow Emmeline,
called the Countess of Ulster, by right of a
former husband, and to his two daughters, Ela
and another Emmeline. Ela was the wife of
Roger le Louche, and had a son Alan. Emmeline was married to one Maurice Fitz
Maurice, but left no issue. Alan, however,
had a daughter and heiress, Matilda, who became the spouse of Robert de Holand. A
grand-daughter of theirs, called Lady Wanborough, brought the place, by marriage, to
John, fifth Baron Lovel of Titchmarsh. This
was in the year 1375. From him descended
Francis, Viscount Lovel, the favourite of

Richard III., of whom more presently. Francis left no issue, and was attainted in 1487. From that year to A.D. 1515 the manor was held by John Cheyne, Knight. Cheyne is a name still known in North Wilts. There is a village ,near Swindon called Rodbourne Cheyne. It is a name known to the readers of Scott. Elspeth in *The Antiquary* sings several old ballads about a gallant Roland Cheyne :

> " To turn the rein were sin and shame,
> To fight were wonderous peril ;
> What would'st thou do now, Roland Cheyne,
> Wert thou Glenallan's earl ? "

Roland Cheyne is all for fighting, though the odds of numbers be immense against them. After Sir John Cheyne, the manor of Wanborough was enjoyed by Sir Edward Darell, of Littlecote. He was owner at the date of his death in 1549. A grandson of his sold it to Sir Humphrey Forster, of Aldermaston, about 1665. Afterwards, in Queen Anne's reign, it was purchased from Sir Charles Hedges by Samuel Sharp, Esq., of Bath.

In the days of Edward I., Sewale d'Oseville and Fitz-Geoffrey were great men at Wanborough. Under them were Foliott, Turnville,

and others.   Wroughton was a name which
had some connection with Wanborough in the
reign of Henry IV.   Brynd is a Wanborough
name.   Thomas Brynd was here in 1665.   He
was the patron of the rectory of Stanton Fitz-
warren.   A Brynd was murdered here in 1571.
J. Goddard had a grant in Wanborough and
Upham in the days of the burly monarch,
Henry VIII.   There is a long list of noble
names, celebrated in their day, which once had
some connection with Wanborough.   How
little is remembered of them there now!   Aubrey
visited Wanborough, as he did so many other
places in North Wilts, nearly two centuries
since, note-book in hand.   Here is a curious
extract from his memoranda :   " Wanboro'.
Here is a Latt Mead celebrated yearly with
great ceremony.   The lord weareth a garland
of flowers ; the mowers at one house have
always a pound of beef and a head of garlic
every man   .   .   .   with many other customs
still retayned.   It is sufficiently well known to
the neighbouring gentry for revelling and horse-
racing."

What was meant by a " Latt Mead " can
now only be conjectured.   It is supposed to

have been a ceremony which originated when Britain was partially a wild, unenclosed, and uncultivated country. The enclosing of a piece of ground would in such times be an event to the neighbourhood, and likely to be commemorated by a festival, or mumming. There are many meadows hereabout known as Lot Meads. The character which Aubrey gives Wanborough is still retained; Wanborough is still a well-known place for revelling, though horse-racing seems to have declined. Aubrey elsewhere mentions a tradition that a moat which was shown him at Wanborough originally surrounded a mansion once inhabited by the famous Francis Lovel, the favourite of Richard III. The mansion had disappeared even then. Who does not remember the rhyme—which, by-the-bye, cost its composer his life :

> " The rat, the cat, and Lovel the dog,
> Rule all England under the Hog,"

alluding to King Richard's crest, which was a boar's head, and to his ministers, Ratcliffe, Catesby, and Lovel. This moat was in a field called Court Close, or Cold Close. A moat, which is supposed to be the same seen by Aubrey, is still very plainly perceivable at Lower Wanborough. It is now dry, and partially surrounds a farmhouse occupied by Mrs. Thorn. A curious discovery was made in the garden of this farmhouse by Mr. H. Thorn, who was digging potatoes, when his spade struck against something, and turned up a quantity of mosaic-work—or what was called mosaic-work—on which the form of a dog was depicted. Beneath this was a leaden coffin, extremely thin, and corroded with age. On being opened it was found to contain a skeleton, supposed to be that of a woman. This has been pronounced a Roman interment by some; others assign it to a later date. Leaden coffins were much used by the Romans, but were not confined to them. This had evidently been in the earth for a great period of time, on account of its extreme thinness; so that the sides fell in on attempting to move it. The teeth in the skull were still perfect. There is a tradition that the moat was once crossed by means of a *copper* (?) drawbridge, close to the entrance to the present farmhouse.

In the memory of man another field, now

WANBOROUGH CHURCH, NEAR SWINDON.

known as the Warnedges, contained ruins, supposed to be those of an ancient mansion. They have now disappeared. They had then an ill name, on account of a murder committed there.

, Wanborough Church is a peculiar structure. It has both a square tower and a spire—one at either end, and of about equal height.[1] It is a very ancient erection. The tower bears the date of 1435—more than four centuries since. The same form of church architecture may be seen at Purton. Wanborough was visited by Captain Symonds, of King Charles's army, in 1644.

After leaving Wanborough, the Faringdon or Wantage road runs along the edge of the down to Hinton, allowing a beautiful view of the Vale of Shrivenham. Hinton Church, some time since, was taken possession of by a swarm of bees, which it was found impossible to dislodge, and so much did the bees annoy the congregation, that service was held in the porch during the summer. From

[1] According to the story, there was a dispute between the two sisters who built the church on the subject of Tower *versus* Spire. This was how they settled it.

Hinton the road winds away to Bishop, or
Bishopstone, a large and pleasant village.
The church contains a remarkably fine arched
door in the chancel, which is of great antiquity. Aubrey came to Bishopstone. He ob-
serves that the church windows were broken by
the soldiers in the Civil Wars—probably by the
army of the Earl of Essex, in its retreat through
Wiltshire towards London. Aubrey also re-
marks that they had here a " Hocker Bench."
How this custom originated, or, indeed, what
it consisted of here, seems unknown—lost in
a dim antiquity. In other places it appears
to have been a kind of game, which consisted
in running after strangers or passers-by, snar-
ing them in a rope, and not allowing them to
proceed until they had paid a forfeit. Here,
also, says Aubrey, was a " Paradise " or Sanc-
tuary—a place wherein it was reported men
were free from arrest. At Bishopstone there
was recently a very ancient mansion, but it
is now pulled down. Bishopstone is a famous
place for ducks and watercress.

Ashbury, the next village, is a very ancient
place. It was formerly spelt Asshebury, and
is mentioned in a Charter of King Edred of

the date 947 A.D., as situated upon the extremity of Ashedoune (now Ashdown), which
then seems to have been the name of a dis-
trict, but is now that of a single down or hill.
Icknield Street (a Roman road) runs through
Ashbury, and winding round the brow of
the adjacent down, passes immediately under
White Horse Hill. It has been conjectured
that the Icknield Street was so named from
being constructed or repaired by the Roman
general Agricola, who was in Britain about
the year 80 A.D., the letters "a" and "g"
being dropped, and the name otherwise cor-
rupted in the course of so many centuries.[1]
At any rate, there can be no doubt that this
road once echoed to the tramp of the Roman
legions.

The next village to Ashbury is Woolston.
It is said that Woolston is a shortened form
of Wulferithstone, a great Saxon chief, who
lived in the days of King Alfred, and was
rewarded for efficient services rendered to that
monarch with the present of some land here-

[1] "Iken.yld.stræt. A Roman road in England, so-called
because it passed through the Iceni, or Norfolk, Suffolk,
etc."—*Bosworth.*

about. Wulferithstone seems to have been
Duke of Hampshire, and to have died A.D.
897. The village of Woolston lies exactly at
the foot of the White Horse Hill, just at the
mouth of that steep-sided, narrow valley which,
commencing below the sculptured form of the
white horse, goes by the name of the White
Horse Manger. This sculptured white horse[1]
is of gigantic size, and is represented at full
gallop. It may be seen fourteen or fifteen
miles off, it being formed by cutting away the
turf down to the white chalk. The length
from the eye to the commencement of the

---

[1] THE WHITE HORSES.

"The *White Horse at Uffington* would appear to be the
great sire and prototype of all. Tradition ascribes it to
Alfred (871).

"*Bratton Hill Horse*, near Westbury. Again ascribed
to Alfred, after Ethandun. Repaired and partially re-cut,
1778. [Also repaired in 1873, at a cost of £40.]

"*Cherhill Horse*, close to reputed Danish camp of Old-
borough, but cut in 1780. The scouring done by the Lord
of the Manor.

"Small horse at *Marlborough*, on the hill behind Pre-
shute. Cut by Mr. Greasley's schoolboys, 1804.

"*Pewsey Valley Horse*, southern slope of Marlborough
Downs, in the parish of Alton Berners. Cut 1812 by John
Harvey. Smaller insignificant horses at Winterbourne Bas-
sett, Roundway Hill (Devizes), and Broad Town, near
Wootton Bassett."—*Wilts Magazine.*

tail is nearly eighty yards, and the tail itself reaches forty-eight yards. Tradition asserts that it was made by order of King Alfred, to commemorate his victory over the Danes at Æscdun, in the year 871. A white horse was the standard of the Saxons, as a raven was that of the Danes. Tacitus relates that the Germans held white horses in the highest veneration, and drew predictions of the future from their neighs or motions; just as the ancient Egyptians did from the bull-god Apis. White horses among the Romans were sacred to the sun. There would be, then, nothing improbable in the Saxons carving the emblem which they bore on their standards as a memorial of their victory. Tradition further states that a custom was instituted of scouring the horse—that is, clearing away the turf which had accumulated once in so many years—a kind of Saxon Olympiad, the length of which appears to be now unknown. Certain it is that the custom has survived until the present day, although performed at very irregular intervals. On such occasions a feast or fair is held in the intrenchment upon the summit of the White Horse Hill. Last time the huge

wagons of Wombwell's Menagerie were dragged
up. A cheese, by tradition, ought to be rolled
down the slope of the White Horse Manger,
to be run down after by those venturesome
enough to risk their necks; but a cart-wheel
was started at the last scouring, and the cheese
preserved whole and sound, to be presented to
the racer who first touched the wheel after its
descent. One of the racers on this occasion,
instead of running, jumped at starting and
rolled headlong down—a most dangerous feat,
which might have cost him his life. Several
other amusing customs used to be put in prac-
tice, which are to be found described at length
in a very pleasant style in the *Scouring of the
White Horse*, a work published some time
since.

Æscdun or Esc'sdune, now Ashdown, was
early a place of importance, as is evident by
its being so frequently mentioned by the old
chroniclers. Ethelwerd alludes to it A.D. 648,
661, and 871. In the year 871, according to
Asser, the Saxons, having been driven from
Reading by the Danes, re-assembled their
forces four days afterwards under King Ethelred and his brother Alfred. The pagan army

of Danes occupied the "higher ground"—
probably the present intrenchment on the
summit of the down—the "Christians," or
Saxons, divided their army into two portions,
one under King Ethelred, and the other
under Alfred. The pagans had also divided
their forces into two; one commanded by
their kings, and the other by five earls. The
Saxons arranged that their king, Ethelred,
should attack the Danish monarchs, and Alfred
the earls. One night is said to have been
spent encamped—the Danes above on Esc's-
dune, or Ashdown, *i.e.* "the hill of the
ash," King Ethelred with his division in
Hardwell Camp, which still remains immediately above Woolston, and is defended by
two fosses. Alfred lay near the present wood
of Ashdown, in a slighter intrenchment, probably thrown up for the occasion; some vestiges
of which still remaining are known as Alfred's
Camp. On the morrow King Ethelred engaged in prayer, and refused to set on until
he had heard mass. Meantime the pagans
poured down the hill, placing Alfred in such
a position that he must either charge without
waiting for his brother or else retreat.

" At length he bravely led his troops against the enemy," entirely unsupported, and Christians and pagans mingled in battle. A single hawthorn tree grew upon the slope—there are some near now—and around this tree was waged the thickest of the battle. It seems to have been undecided until Ethelred, having finished his devotions, came up with his followers, when the Danes were immediately routed, and fled towards Reading. "All the flower of the barbarian youth was there slain," says Ethelwerd, "so that never before nor since was ever such destruction known since the Saxons gained Britain by their arms." There fell of the Danes, King Bagsac, Earl Sidrac the elder, and Earl Sidrac the younger, Earl Osbern, Earl Frene, and Earl Harold.

Away to the east of White Horse Hill, the direction in which the battle rolled, may still be seen seven barrows, supposed to be the burial-places of those who fell in the engagement. Close behind the Ridge Way road, about a mile from the brow of Ashdown, may be seen a cromlech, by some thought to be the sepulchre of the above-mentioned King Bag-

ENTRANCE TO SWINDON FROM COATE.

sac ; it being a Danish custom to inter their nobility in such a manner. This monument is now hidden in a beech-copse, and consists of three stones set on edge, supporting a fourth— a broad covering-stone. More are scattered round, forming an oval. Altogether, there are now about thirty stones here which are visible. It has much the appearance of an altar. Sacrifices may have been offered to the deceased Dane. Some think it a work of the Druids. It is evidently very ancient, being mentioned in a Saxon charter as a landmark. The country people call it Wayland Smith's cave, and tell a story of an invisible smith, who shoed travellers' horses, on condition of their laying a groat upon the altar-stone, and then retiring out of sight—whistling when hid, as a signal, and leaving the horse near. Presently there would be a tinkling of hammers, and on returning to the spot the horse would be found shod and no one in sight. This legend came under the notice of Sir Walter Scott, who is said to have visited the place. He has embodied it in the novel of *Kenilworth*. The legend is thought to have originated in a Danish superstition concerning

K

spirits who dwelt in rocks, and were cunning workmen in iron and steel.

The memory of King Alfred still lies here. His bugle-horn is shown at a wayside inn called the "Blowing-Stone," about a mile from the White Horse Hill. It is a large Sarsden, with many holes, one of which, being blown through, causes a noise which may be heard at a great distance.

Uffington, a village near by, is thought to be a corruption of Ubba's meadow-town. Ubba, or Offa, was a celebrated king in the time of the Heptarchy. Some have supposed it to be Glevum, a Roman station mentioned in the Itineraries.

Immediately beneath the figure of the horse is a conical mound, or barrow, known as the Dragon's mound; from a tradition that here St. George slew the dragon, whose blood was of so poisonous a nature that nothing has since grown upon its summit, which is bare, exposing the chalk. Here, so it is supposed, fell one of the Pen-dragons of the British, their chief of chiefs, whom their ordinary kings elected to lead them against the Saxons, and whose name, abridged of the "pen," may have had some share in the legend. Natan-leod, or Nazan-leod, a name meaning the same as Pen-dragon, was slain in these parts, say the chroniclers, with 5,000 British under him, about the year 550, by Cedric the Saxon. This barrow may have been raised over his remains, as was the British custom.

Wantage, formerly Wanating, was the birth-place of the renowned King Alfred, who was born here, according to Asser, in 849—over a thousand years ago. It was a royal residence then. The Saxon palace stood on a place called High Garden. Roman remains have been found at Wantage in a place known as Limborough. Coins also have been found there. In the last century a place was dis-covered to which the name of "Alfred's cellar" was given. It was bricked, and appeared to have been a bath. Wherever the Romans went, there they built baths, if it were possible. In a place like Wantage—whose hero is Alfred—anything that savoured of antiquity would be ascribed to that renowned monarch. Wantage is in Berks, "which county," writes Asser, " has its name from the wood of Berroc, where the box tree grows most abundantly."

CHAPTER VI

THE MARLBOROUGH ROAD

THERE are two distinct roads from Swindon to Marlborough, on both of which may be found objects of antiquarian interest, one known as Marlborough Lane, the other as Coate Road. Coate is at a distance of about a mile and a half from the town, and has been much visited on account of the reservoir. The etymology of the name would seem to make it a place of considerable antiquity, being probably derived from the Anglo-Saxon cot, a cottage, or dwelling-place. In Percy's *Reliques of Ancient Poetry* there is an old ballad written by Michael Drayton, and published about 1592, in one of his Pastorals, which contains the following verse. The ballad is called "Dowsabell," and a shepherd-swain is complaining of the coldness of his fair one :

MARLBOROUGH LANE, SWINDON.

> "My coate, sayeth he, nor yet my foulde
> Shall neither sheep nor shepheard hould,
>   Except thou favour me."

The glossary affixed to the end of the volume has " Coate, cot, or cottage." The spelling, it will be observed, is identical with that by which the village is now represented. The " coate," or cot, was the residence of the " shepheard." His pathetic appeal was not unsuccessful :—

> "With that she bent her snow-white knee
> Downe by the shepheard kneeled shee,
>   And him she sweetely kist ;
> With that the shepheard whooped for joy,
> Quoth he, ' Ther's never shepheard's boy,
>   That ever was so blist.' "

The broad country pronunciation, however, makes it Cawt, which does not sound like Cot, or Cote. This more approaches the Welsh word cwt, a hovel. Now the Welsh language is that of the ancient Britons. If this derivation be correct, Coate would date back to them.[1] There is some reason for supposing

---

[1] Though hitherto "unknown to fame," future students of English literature will not be likely to forget that Richard Jefferies was born, and lived the greater part of his life, at Coate.

that the village was once more extensive than
at present, and that it could show a church.
From time immemorial a cow-pen upon land
in the occupation of Mr. H. Brunsden has
gone by the name of church-pen. The reason
is obvious. Here are six pillars about eight
feet high, by two in diameter, circular, and
formed of hewn stone. At present they simply
support the roof of a shed ; but it does not
seem probable that such substantial pillars were
originally erected for this purpose. They are
nearly east and west. Bones, it is said, have
been dug up in the adjacent ground, but such
testimony is very unreliable until examined by
a person learned in anatomy. The road from
Coate makes a wide semi-circle round to Chisledon. Day-house Lane cuts off the angle, and
was formerly much used, until the road was
widened and macadamised. There may be
seen on the left side of Day-house Lane,
exactly opposite the entrance to a pen on Day-
house Farm,[1] five Sarsden stones, much sunk
in the ground, but forming a semi-circle of
which the lane is the base-line or tangent.

---

[1] The early home of Richard Jefferies' wife.

A. G. Taylor

DAY HOUSE FARM, COATE.

There was a sixth upon the edge of the lane,
but it was blown up and removed, in order to
make the road more serviceable, a few years
ago. Whether this was or was not one of
those circles known as Druidical, cannot now be
determined, but it wears that appearance. It
would seem that the modern lane had cut right
through the circle, destroying all vestige of one
half of it. In the next field, known as the
Plain, lies, near the footpath across the fields to
Chisledon, another Sarsden of enormous size,
with two smaller satellites of the same stone
close by. If the semi-circle just spoken of
was a work of the Druids, or of the description known as Druidical, which some think a
very different thing, it may be just possible
that these detached stones in the Plain had
some connection with it.

A little further up the same line is a place
known as Badbury Wick. Wick is an old
Saxon word having a loose meaning, but generally indicating a habitation. Here, on the
left-hand in a field, there are deep and wide
grass-grown fosses, having a remarkable likeness to a moat. A moat does not of necessity
denote the position of a fortified building. In

Roman Catholic times—three centuries since
and more—when fish was the diet of all who
could get it at certain periods of the year, a
moat would answer a double purpose—that of
defence, and that of a fish pond. Badbury
lies partly upon the side of a hill and partly in
a deep valley. There is a large elm tree in
the middle of the village ; here stood the stocks
within the memory of man, and a small portion
still remains. Badbury is a very ancient village, and dates from the Saxon times at least.
One enthusiastic antiquarian of the last century
was of the opinion that here, or upon the hill
immediately above it—well known as Liddington Hill and famous for its camp—was the
identical spot where the renowned King Arthur
won his twelfth battle in the year 520, or
thereabout. If this conjecture be true, Badbury was a known place more than thirteen
centuries since. According to Nennius,[1] the
ancient British historian, it was even longer
ago than this. About the middle of the fifth

---

[1] Nennius, the supposed author of *Historia Britonum*,
bringing the chronicle to 655 A.D. He is said to have been
a Welsh monk at Bangor, but all so-called facts about him
are open to as much question as is his history.

century he writes thus : " There it was that the magnanimous Arthur, with all the kings and military force of Britain, fought against the Saxons.[1] And although there were many more noble than himself, yet he was twelve times their commander, and was as often conqueror." Giving the places where he was victorious in eleven battles, Nennius proceeds : " The twelfth battle was a severe contest, when Arthur penetrated to the hill of Badon. In this engagement, nine hundred and forty fell by his hand alone, no one but the Lord affording him assistance." A wonderful feat, equalling that which Samson executed upon the Philistines. This "hill of Badon," or "mons Badonicus," has perhaps caused more discussion and disagreement than any other single doubtful point in the early history of England. Some unhesitatingly place it at Bath ; Baydonhill near Aldbourne has had its claims put forward ; others prefer Badbury, it being a place of undoubted antiquity, and in the immediate neighbourhood of places very celebrated in days gone by. Nor is King Arthur

---

[1] Under Cerdic (?).

the only personage of antiquity with whom
Badbury has been in some degree connected.
Who has not heard of St. Dunstan ? Dunstan,[1]
Abbot of Glastonbury—whose saintship is so
much doubted, and whose fame approaches in-
famy. Dunstan first became celebrated in the
reign of King Edred, in about the middle of
the tenth century. Edred's reign ended in the
year 955. He gave in the same year the
manor of Badbury to St. Dunstan. A charter
is said to be still preserved, containing the
boundaries. It mentions the " Ten Stones" as
a landmark. Much later, the Ridforms, or
Ridferns, became lords of the manor. A
monument to one of them was in Chisledon
church.

Chisledon, which lies somewhat to the right
of the Marlborough road, is a very ancient
village. There is a place here known as Black-
man's barrow ; and barrows are considered to
be the burial places of the Britons. A Roman
road—the Skelton Way—passes through the
place, as does also a British track, known as
the " Rudgeway," that is, the Ridge Way, or

---

[1] Dunstan, b. 925, d. 988.

road running along the ridge of the hills. The
Ridge Way branches off from the Skineld
Street at Streetly, passes by White-Horse Hill,
and, after leaving Chisledon, runs to Avebury.
It was probably the ancient military road con-
necting the fortifications upon the downs with
each other. On the north of Chisledon frowns
Liddington Castle, a well-preserved earthwork
upon the brow of the hill. On the south, at a
greater distance, may be seen another entrenchment, that of Barbury. The downs fall back,
forming a semi-circle through which the Marlborough road passes, by means of a vale and
pass at Ogbourne, and thus enclose a wide plain
—a most fit and proper place for a town in ancient times. Here accordingly stands Chisledon,
on the very edge of the plain, giving the inhabitants the vantage ground of the hill in case of
attack from the vale beneath. The etymology
of the name shows its great antiquity; Ceasel-
dene—ceasel is an Anglo-Saxon word for
gravel, sand, or rubble, of which there is a
sufficiency at Chisledon, and dene, meaning
plain. Hence Ceasel-dene would mean perhaps the gravel or rubble plain, and the name
of the plain would be quickly applied to the

village upon it.   The Saxon *ce*, has in several
instances been changed into *ch*, in the lapse of
centuries.   A familiar example is the word
churl—meaning a rude, uncivil fellow, a rustic
—derived from the Saxon word laborer, or serf,
rude as the soil he cultivated.   Charles [1] is said
to have come from the same root, meaning a
husbandman.   Chisledon Church was visited by
Aubrey two centuries since.   Here are his
memoranda concerning it :—

" By the communion table a gravestone of
marble, with brasses, with this inscription :
' Here lyeth the body of Francis Rutland,
Esquier, sonne and heir to Nycolas Rutland of
Micham in the countie of Surrie esquier, who
marryed the daughter of Thomas Stephens
esqr., and had four sonnes and two daughters.
He died XXVII of August, 1592.'   The
escutcheon's lost : he was a courtier and died
in the progress.

" In nave ecclesiæ : ' Here lieth the body of
Rich. Harvey gentlemen, who departed this

---

[1] "Charles, originally man, male—akin to A. S. *ceorl*,
freeman of the lowest rank, man, husband ; and perhaps to
Skr. *jāra*, lover."— *Webster*.

CHISLEDON CHURCH, NEAR SWINDON.

life January 16 and was buried Jan. —— 1668 æt suæ 80.'"

Francis Rutland, esquire, who "was a courtier and died in the progress," was probably one of the court of Queen Elizabeth, and died ‚whilst accompanying her in one of her annual journeys through her dominions. Stephens is a name that was formerly connected with Burderop. There is a tradition that Queen Elizabeth slept a night or two at a mansion at Upper Upham, about two miles from Chisledon. The Calleys of Burderop have their family vaults in the church. The name was well known in the time of the Civil Wars. On the death-warrant of Charles I. is the signature of "Will Cawley." He was for a long while considered the ancestor of the present owner of Burderop, but this has been shown to have arisen from a mistake, the "Will Cawley" named above belonging to another family. Chisledon can still show a stocks in first-rate order, and perfectly capable of confining a malefactor, should that ancient mode of punishment ever come again into use. They stand immediately beneath the churchyard wall, close to the gate; a pleasant situation for an incarcerated offender, especially upon a Sunday.

The Ridge Way road when it leaves Chisledon winds away to Draycott Foliatt. Here there once stood a church, but it has disappeared, and a part of the woodwork was probably used in building an adjacent house. The churchyard may still be seen—no building is allowed to be erected upon it—and bones were dug up when a saw-pit was being made there. A clergyman still receives a stipend from the inhabitants of Draycott, and preaches a sermon once a year in the adjoining church of Chisledon in return. Leaving Draycott Foliatt, the Ridge Way—now broad, and only shown to be a road by the waggon tracks on the turf—runs under Barbury Castle. Here in days gone by was Burderop racecourse. Silver cups which were won upon this springy turf are still preserved here and there about the country. Burderop Races were celebrated in former days. Now the greater portion of the course is ploughed up, and the remainder occupied by furze.

Upon the summit of Barbury may be seen one of those numerous camps or entrenchments scattered about at various points upon the downs. This is a peculiar one. It consists of two fosses, or ditches, one within the other. If we remember rightly, such was the Saxon method of encampment ; but it by no means follows that Barbury Castle was originally fortified by them. In all probability these posts, known as castles, have been successively occupied by Briton, Anglo-Saxon, Roman, and Dane ; each and all of whom altered the form of the fortification to suit their peculiar requirements, so that each camp would bear the outline given it by its last occupants. The inner fosse here is very deep, and its sides are nearly perpendicular—it was carried deeper and was cut more steep than that at Liddington, though the ground enclosed may not be so extensive. The outer fosse is by no means so broad. It must have required a large number of men to defend such fortifications as these, and especially in times when fighting was carried on hand to hand—when every foot of ground would be occupied by a warrior. It is very evident that these fortifications were constructed before missile weapons were employed. Here is no attempt at flanking. The defenders

have no advantage excepting those of two deep
ditches, and an embankment between them and
the assailants.   They cannot deliver a cross
fire.   They must stand face to face, and hand
to hand, and side by side all along the edge of
these embankments.   Nor must the fosses be
left empty.   The defenders of such a fortification in those days would need to be counted by
thousands.   But where could thousands of
warriors be got from?   North Wilts could not
supply, or certainly could not spare them
now.

Nor is this the only camp in this part of the
country.   Look away to the north-east.   Two
may be seen in a line with each other and with
Barbury, capping the crown of the hills.   They
are Liddington and White Horse Hills.   There
is a general impression that in ancient days
Britain was a mere wild waste, unpeopled, one
vast extent of forest and mountain.   This certainly was not the case with North Wilts and
that part of Berks joining its north-eastern extremity.   The place, so to say, is literally alive
with the dead.   Not a step can be taken which
does not lead to some token of antiquity.   Turn
up the turf and you shall find coins, arrow-

heads, and bones. Walk in the fields and you shall see the traces of moats and ancient buildings. Ascend the downs and pause in astonishment before the vast fortifications of a former era. These downs were once trodden by the bold Britons; the Roman soldier lay down to rest upon the thymy turf; the Saxon stretched himself at ease on yonder embankment; the Dane imbrued his weapon in the blood of the Saxon on yonder hill. North Wilts must have been as populous then as now, the difference being simply in the change of the spots inhabited.

Barbury has been considered to have been the scene of a terrible battle, recorded in the ancient Chronicles. Ethelwerd writes thus :—
" A.D. 552, Cenric,[1] fought against the Britons near the town of Scarburh (Old Sarum, near Salisbury), and having routed them, slew a large number. The same, some years after (559), fought with Ceawlin against the Britons near a place called Berin-byrig." Berin-byrig certainly might in the course of centuries become changed to Barbury. It would

---

[1] Or Cynric.

L

merely require the dropping of the second syllable, "in," and the broadening of the vowel *e*. The letter *g* is properly *y*. Cenric and Ceawlin were two Saxon chiefs. If this be a true conjecture, Barbury Castle or camp has probably been in existence for more than thirteen hundred years ; and yet it is still in a condition which might, in an emergency, afford a good shelter to a considerable garrison, and will probably remain thus whilst the hill stands. These works of the ancient inhabitants of Britain were by no means so slight and insignificant as has been supposed. It must have required an enormous amount of labour to dig out these deep fosses, more especially with the tools of that day. Probably much of the earth was carried up in baskets. The Ridge Way runs from Barbury away to Avebury. At the foot of the hill close to the Marlborough road stand two tumuli. Tumuli accompany the Ridge Way the whole course of its length. It was not a method of burial singular to the Britons. Homer makes mention of tumuli. Hector offers single combat to the Grecians in the Iliad, promising should he be successful to restore the dead body of his assailant :—

" Whilst to his friends restored, funereal rites
  The sorrowing Grecians at their ships perform :
  And on the Hellespont's resounding shore
  Erect the tumulus that future times
  May know, and late posterity remark,
  Ploughing the briny wave ; Behold the tomb
  Of some illustrious chief by Hector slain !
  So shall my glory brave the wreck of years."

The British chiefs, or whoever they may be that lie buried at the foot of Barbury, have not been so fortunate as Hector. Their glory has not braved the wreck of years. Their very names are unknown. Conjecture itself can go no further than to suppose that the bodies of those slain in the battle with Cenric and Ceawlin lie here. They had no Homer. Richard of Cirencester, describing the funeral rites of the ancient Britons, proceeds thus :—
" Their interments were magnificent ; and all the things which they prized during life, even arms and animals, were thrown into the funeral pile. A heap of earth and turf formed the sepulchre." Here there is another analogy with the customs of the Greeks, as recorded by Homer. At Patroclus's funeral, after certain ceremonies,—

> " Then in the pyle
> Four generous steeds they cast still groaning loud ;
> And add to these two of nine faithful dogs,
> Whilom their master's care ! "

—" the things which they prized during life " of the Cirencester chronicler.

When Burderop races were run immediately beneath the slope of the hill, Barbury was covered with spectators, but at present the hill is deserted, save by the flint-diggers, the shepherds, and an occasional traveller. Burderop can be distinctly seen at a distance of two good miles. Adjoining Burderop is a place called Hodson—a small village which, like the towns of the Britons, is situated in a wood. Hodson is said to have been formerly spelt Hoddesdon, and, if so, may be the place alluded to in the following verse of a sonnet which may be found in *Laura ; or, Select Sonnets and Quartorzans*, published early in the present century. The same work contains a sonnet written after walking across the Marlborough Downs to Midenhall, on a stormy night. The sonnet is addressed to the pimpernel :—

> " Gem of the fields, whose form and hues first gave
> The sense of beauty to my childish eye,

If many a traveller pass unheeding by,
To me thou wilt not in oblivion's wave
Sink ; could my muse thy beauteous flow'rets lave
In brightest tints of immortality
Thou hast deserved.   Whate'er on earth or sky
Wafts the delighted thought beyond the grave.

From such beginning dawned upon the mind
What time my infant feet on Hoddesdon's ground
First learnt to pace.   With what new joy I saw
Thine azure eye with golden summits crowned
And scarlet leaves, which coming tempests bind
Cinquefolded close, warm suns to fair expansion draw."

September 9th, 1805.   C. L.

A note added states that the country name
of the pimpernel is wincopipe, probably from
" wind, go pipe," the closing of the flower being
a well-known sign of tempest.

Perhaps two miles from Barbury, upon the
Marlborough road, is a small village—actually
without a public-house—called Ruckley.   On
the down above this place there are a number
of Sarsden stones.   Nine of these seem to
form an oval, and there are four more within,
placed two by two.   This may be another of
those works commonly ascribed to the Druids.
The ends of the oval point nearly east and
west.   Marlborough race ground is immediately

beneath this hill.   Some distance further is a
place known as the " Devil's Den " [1] among
the country people, where are a number of
stones, and amongst them two of great height,
placed on end, with a third across, like a beam,
forming a kind of portal.   It may be observed
that the so-much admired Grecian architecture
in its severest form was but an ornamental im-
provement upon this simple erection : the
pillars were fluted, and capitals added, but the
idea was the same in the Druidical temples,
such as Stonehenge.   The arch seems to have
come from the Goths.   Not a great distance
from the " Devil's Den " is a place known as
Temple Bottom, where were a number of
stones, which of late years have been broken
up and removed.   Hewish,[2] near which these
remains of a period which preceded history
may be seen, is a place which became known
to the London reading public through the
medium of No. 237 of *Household Words*, published Saturday, October 7th, 1867.   In that
number may be found a most amusing article

---

[1] " A cromlech or dolmen."—*Worth.*
[2] Hewish Hill bears traces of having been a British
village.

headed "The Ghost of Pit Pond." The writer takes up his residence at Marlborough, at the "Castle" Inn, which was then famous for roast capons, and while amusing himself by strolling over the adjacent downs he meets with an old shepherd, and from him learns several legends, amongst which "The Ghost of Pit Pond, Hewish," occupies the most space. The action takes place about fifty years previous to the writer's arrival at Marlborough, which was twenty years ago ; consequently it must have been nearly a century since. A Mr. Reeves, of Hewish Farm, says the legend, hung himself for the love of an equestrian actress, whose wonderful horsemanship he had seen displayed in a leap of twenty-five feet. The ghost of the suicide being reported to walk, a clergyman was called in, and the spirit laid in Pit Pond close by, which previously was clear as crystal, but immediately afterwards became muddy and green, nor would the beasts drink from it. The shepherd finishes his tale by remarking that "You may believe I haven't told you a word but what's been told to me for true."

Marlborough lies a short distance from Ruckley. The following extract is from Lord

Clarendon's History of the Great Rebellion, and relates to the siege of Marlborough during the Civil Wars.

" The king was hardly settled in his quarters (at Oxford) when he heard that the Parliament was fixing a garrison at Marlborough in Wiltshire, a town the most notoriously disaffected of all that county ; otherwise, saving the obstinacy and malice of the inhabitants, in the situation of it very unfit for a garrison. Thither the Earl of Essex had sent one Ramsay (a Scotchman, as most of their officers were of that nation), to be governor, who, with the help of the factious people there, had quickly drawn together five or six hundred men. This place the king saw would quickly prove an ill neighbour to him, not only as it was in the heart of a rich county, and so would straiten, and even infect, his quarters (for it was within twenty miles of Oxford), but as it did cut off his line of communication with the west, and therefore, though it was December, a season when his tired and almost naked soldiers might expect rest, he sent a strong party of horse, foot, and dragoons, under the command of Mr. Wilmott, the lieutenant-general of horse, to visit that

JEFFERIES' HOUSE, COATE.

town ; who, coming thither on a Saturday, found the place strongly mann'd ; for, besides the garrison, it being market-day, very many country people came thither to buy and sell, and were all compell'd to stay and take arms for the defence of the place ; which, for the most part, they were willing to do, and the people peremptory to defend it. Though there was no line about it, yet there was some place of great advantage upon which they had raised batteries and planted cannon, and so barricadoed all the avenues, which were through deep narrow lanes, that the horse could do little service.

" When the lieutenant-general was with his party near the town, he apprehended a fellow who confessed upon examination that he was a spy, and sent by the governor to bring intelligence of their strength and motion. When all men thought, and the poor fellow himself fear'd, he should be executed, the lieutenant-general caused his whole party to be ranged in order in the next convenient place, and bid the fellow look well upon them and observe them, and then bid him return to the town, and tell those that sent him what he had seen, and

withal that he should acquaint the magistrates
of the town that they should do well to tract
with the garrison to give them leave to submit
to the king ; that if they did so, the town
should not receive the least prejudice ; but if
they compell'd him to make his way, and enter
the town by force, it would not be in his power
to keep his soldiers from taking that which
they should win with their blood ; and so dis-
miss'd him.   This generous act proved of some
advantage ; for the fellow, transported with
having his life given him, and the numbers of
the men he had seen (besides his no experience
in such sights), being multiplied by his fear,
made notable relations of the strength, gal-
lantry, and resolution of the enemy, and of
the impossibility of resisting them ; which,
though it prevailed not with those in authority
to yield, yet it strangely abated the hopes and
courage of the people.   So that when the
king's soldiers fell on, after a volley or two, in
which much execution was done, they threw
down their arms, and ran into the town ; so
that the foot had time to make room for the
horse, who were now entered at both ends of
the town, yet were not so near an end as they

expected ; for the streets were in many places barricadoed, which were obstinately defended by some soldiers and townsmen, who killed many men out of the windows of the houses ; so that, it may be, if they had trusted only to their own strength, without compelling the countrymen to increase their number, and who, being first frighted and weary, disheartened their companions, that place might have cost more blood. Ramsey, the governor, was himself retired into the church with some officers, and from thence did some hurt ; upon this, there being so many kill'd out of windows, fire was put to the next houses, so that a good part of the town was burn'd, and then the soldiers enter'd, doing less execution than could reasonably be expected, but what they spared in blood they took in pillage, the soldiers inquiring little who were friend or foes.

" This was the first garrison taken on either side (for I cannot call Farnham Castle in Surrey one, whither some gentlemen who were willing to appear for the king had repaired, and were taken with less resistance than was fit, by Sir William Waller some few days before it deserved the name of a garrison) ; in which were taken (besides the governor and other officers, who yielded upon quarter), above one thousand prisoners, great store of arms, four pieces of canon, and a good quantity of amunition, with all which the lieutenant-general returned safe to Oxford."

CHAPTER VII

THE DEVIZES ROAD

THE first place of interest to an antiquarian upon the Devizes road from
Swindon is the village of Wroughton, about
three miles distant. It is the largest village in
the neighbourhood, and is placed in a most
beautiful situation. Wood, water, dell and
down, combine to render it a most attractive
spot. Recently the operations of the Swindon
Water Works' Company have completely
altered the aspect of one of the romantic
valleys of which there are several in the neighbourhood of Wroughton; but the memory of
the Seven Springs will not quickly die away
from the remembrance of its inhabitants.
Wroughton has long retained its celebrity as
a beautiful place. Aubrey, who came here two
hundred years ago, says that around here was

the garden of Wiltshire, meaning to intimate
its fertility and high state of cultivation. It is
an ancient place. Some say that one of the
downs immediately over the village was originally called Ellandune. Ellandune was once
the scene of a severe contest. The Chronicle
of Ethelwerd contains the following passage :—
"A.D. 823 . . . King Egbert fought a
battle against Burnulf, King of the Mercians,
at Ellandune, and Egbert gained the victory ;
but there was a great loss on both sides ; and
Hun, duke of the Province of Somerset, was
there slain ; he lies buried in the city of Winchester. Egbert was king of the West Saxons,
and became a very celebrated monarch." This
battle took place over a thousand years ago, in
which time great changes might be expected to
occur in the names of spots once well known as
the scenes of strife, and a consequent difficulty
to arise in fixing their exact situation. Hence
Ellandune has been also considered to be near
Wilton. If the battle really did take place
near Wroughton, upon a down called Ellandune, it was probably at no great distance from
the spot where the church now stands. The
vale beneath still goes by the name of Ell-

comb, in which is preserved the first syllable of
Ellandune. "En" has been frequently dropped
in the course of centuries, as Oxenford, Oxford.
Comb would seem to come from an ancient
British word, still preserved in the Welsh
‚cwm, meaning a vale. Ellcomb would naturally
be the vale beneath Ellandune. This is,
however, merely a conjecture. Wroughton
churchyard is remarkably crowded with grave-
stones, which cluster so closely around an
ancient yew that its stem can scarcely be seen.
The support of a sundial still remains, but
the gnomon and hour-circle have disappeared.
Close by the portal is a tombstone with the
following curious inscription :—

"John Dvcke, departed this life the 16th day August, 1666,
Who lived well to die never, and died well to live ever."

Broad Hinton is the next village. By the
side of the road thither, there may be observed
crosses cut deep into the turf, and kept clean
by the roadmenders, in order to commemorate
the spots where accidents or murders have
taken place. Broad Hinton is on the plain
beneath the swelling downs. Here may be
seen cut out on the turf, on the slope of the

down, close beside the Marlborough road, another white horse, though of far less size than that at Ashdown. These horses are far from uncommon upon the Marlborough Downs, and may, perhaps, indicate the strong hold which the Saxons had gained upon this part of Britain. Besides this, there is the celebrated white horse at Ashdown, and the almost equally well known white horse at Marlborough, which the scholars take a delight in cleaning—three, perhaps, within ten miles of each other. Broad Hinton has its legend as well as other better known places. Somewhat apart from the village stands a magnificent yew-tree, and near by it a cottage. Part of this cottage is built over a large well of enormous depth, the chain to which the two buckets are attached, one going up as the other goes down, is said to be two hundred feet in length. The chain runs over a shaft, turned by a large wheel, which can be set revolving by a man standing within it—a giddy operation to those unused to such exertion. A testimony to the depth of the well is easily obtained by dropping a stone down, when several moments elapse ere it touches the water, causing a noise which, reverberating from the sides, resembles thunder. At the bottom of this well lies wealth in the shape of plate, says tradition. This plate, according to the same authority, was thrown down here in the time of the Civil War. So strong is the belief amongst the common people of the truth of this story that some men, no great while since, offered to undertake the arduous work of cleaning it out, for what they would find at the bottom—which offer was, however, declined by the owner, who considered the operation too dangerous. Near by this cottage the ground is uneven and irregular, generally a sure sign of having once been built upon, and accordingly here, says tradition, once stood a noble mansion known as Broad Hinton House.

Broad Hinton Church is a very ancient erection.[1] It was visited by Aubrey in the seventeenth century, who therein copied an inscription which time has now rendered nearly illegible, though sufficient remains to identify

---

[1] The modern glass in this ancient church deserves notice.

the monument to which he refers. It is upon
the north side of the chancel, facing the communion table, and consists of a slab let into
the wall. Here is Aubrey's copy :—

" Here lyeth Syr William Wroughton,
knight, who dyed in the 50 yeare of his age
in Anno Dom. 1559 ; and left jssewe of his
body by Dame Elinor his wife, daughter of
Edward Lewknor, esq., 4 sonnes and 3
daughters; and built the house at Broad-
hinton, Anno Domini 1540."

This house at Broad Hinton, built by Syr
William Wroughton, is undoubtedly the same
of which tradition says that it stood near the
well above-mentioned, which well was probably
dug to supply it with water, so necessary in
those days, when no one knew how soon it
might be before his house would be besieged.
Syr William Wroughton flourished in the reign
of Henry the Eighth, and built his house
whilst that monarch sat upon the throne,
though he did not die until the first year of
Queen Elizabeth. Those were stirring times.
In the fifty years of his life, Syr William
Wroughton had seen four occupants of the
throne—Henry the Eighth, Edward the Sixth,

Queen Mary and, lastly, Queen Elizabeth.
He could have related, no doubt, the rumours
of Henry's cruelty and love of change—witness
thereto his many wives ; of Edward's piety, of
the persecution of the reformers by Queen
Mary, and of the glory of the nation after the
accession of Elizabeth. He could remember
the short reign of Lady Jane Grey, and her
unfortunate end. Syr William Wroughton
lived in dangerous days, and doubtless had his
share in the convulsions which agitated England. Wroughton is an ancient name. Persons bearing it held property at Wanborough
in times long gone by. Other members of the
family lie buried in Broad Hinton church. On
the opposite side of the chancel there is a
monument, said to be that of Syr Thomas
Wroughton, son of the Syr William mentioned
above. A figure of the knight, somewhat
under full size, kneels upon a cushion, facing
the altar, as if praying, though the hands are
now broken off. He is in armour. Immediately behind him kneels his lady, wearing a
head-covering of the most extraordinary shape.
To-day satire is directed against the feminine
sex on account of the small size of their

bonnets, neither defending the head against
wind nor rain ; then the case was precisely the
reverse. Fashions in their changes often revert to those of times gone by. Pray heaven
the fickle goddess of fashion may never startle
the affrighted world by reproducing the head-
covering of Lady Wroughton! Over the
knight and his lady is a kind of canopy, and
beneath them small carved figures of their
eight children—four boys, and as many girls ;
the boys beneath their father, the girls beneath
their mother.

Broad Hinton estate formerly belonged to
the Wroughton family, from whom it was purchased by Sir John Glanville, second son of
John Glanville, Judge, P.C., in 1640. He was
a very celebrated Sergeant-at-Law, and still
more famous as the Speaker of the House of
Commons during the agitation which preceded
the Civil War. He is mentioned by Lord
Clarendon in his History of the Rebellion.
Glanville, says tradition, burned Broad Hinton
House, in order to prevent its being used as a
garrison by the Parliament.[1] If there be any

---

[1] And afterwards lived in the gatehouse.

truth in the tale, it was probably at this time that the plate which has already been alluded to was cast down the well, that it might not be seized by the Parliamentarian soldiers, and converted into the means of carrying on the war against King Charles. There are several monuments to the Glanville family in Broad Hinton church. On the left side of the chancel, facing the altar, stands a full-length statue of one of them in armour, and holding a gilded staff in one hand, the end of the staff resting upon his thigh. The crest is a stag. This statue is of alabaster, and well executed. The date is A.D. 1645—the days of King Charles and the Civil War—and there is a long Latin inscription running up the wall on each side of the statue, in a most awkward manner for the reader. Sir John Glanville, eldest son of the famous Sergeant-at-Law, was a lieutenant in the service of King Charles the First, and died at the siege of Bridgewater, in Somerset, in 1645. Beyond the monument and inscription to Syr William Wroughton, on the same side of the chancel, is a monument to the memory of Johannes Glanville, son of John Glanville, of Tavistock. He lived temp.

Charles I. and II. The date is 1661. Near
by is another monument to another Glanville,
dated 1673. Here is suspended high up, immediately beneath the roof, a large helmet,
with a pair of gauntlets, somewhat mutilated,
as if they had seen service, and been where

> "With many a thwack, and many a bang,
>   Hard crabtree and old iron rang."

The Glanville crest was evidently a stag,
miniature representations of which can be seen
in numerous places. The coat-of-arms of the
Wroughtons interred here bears three boars'
heads, whose tusks can still be seen, though
they have been sculptured here these three
centuries and more.

John Evelyn once came to Broad Hinton.
His memoirs have been since published, and
contain much amusing matter concerning the
court of Charles II. Sir John Evelyn (?) was
a person so deeply implicated in the rebellion
that he was excepted by name in King
Charles's proclamation of pardon to Wiltshire,
according to Lord Clarendon.

Some distance beyond Broad Hinton lies
Avebury, a place which is perhaps the most

fertile spot in objects of antiquarian interest of any in North Wilts. Avebury is best approached—that is for a view—by the Ridg Way road, which runs there along the ridge or summit of the downs from Barbury. From 'the last down, Avebury,[1] or, as it is more usually spelt and written, Abury, can be seen to great advantage. Probably to a stranger it would be invisible, however, the village being concealed by trees, and a vast mound of earth thrown up which surrounds it. Abury is in the middle of a plain, and seems to have been approached by an avenue of stones much more than a mile in length. A similar approach to the temples of their gods marked the Egyptian places of worship, although in their case, the

---

[1] "Aubrey has strong claims upon us touching Avebury, for he 'discovered' it in an accidental view during a hunting excursion in 1648, and he returned to its study again and again. It was fortunate that he did so, for the character of the monument was unnoticed in the only previous record, Holland's *Camden*; and he has left us accurate descriptions and plans as in the day when he took 'this old, ill-shapened monument to be the greatest, most considerable, and least ruinated of any of the kind in our British isle.' '*Most* ruinated' as it now is, without his help a very inadequate idea could be formed of its pristine character."—*R. N. Worth.*

stones instead of being merely placed on end were carved into the likeness of sphinxes, many of which remain to this day to testify to the grandeur with which the Egyptian priests surrounded their mysterious religion. The stone avenue at Abury commences on the slope at the entrance to a deep-sided narrow valley east of the village, and does not simply consist of two rows of stones : nor is the appearance of regularity always visible, nor invariably preserved during the whole distance. At the commencement of the avenue the stones seem scattered about without any attempt at order ; in a short distance they assume a more regular appearance, being placed upon the bottom of the valley.[1] Here and there lie as many as three or four huge stones, thrown almost one upon the other, and partially overlapping. These would seem to have been originally cromlechs—stones set on edge and covered in with one broad flat stone. That this was the case appears to be still more evident in other stone groups, where the cromlechs seem to

[1] Avebury, like Stonehenge, possesses a literature of its own, from which the reader can expand the somewhat meagre details mentioned by Jefferies.

have sunk bodily into the earth, though still
sufficiently above ground to enable their original position to be conjectured. If these were
cromlechs they probably served the double
purpose of at once forming a monument to
'some departed worthy of renown, and at the
same time that of an altar for sacrificing to his
manes or spirit, as seems to have been the
custom amongst numerous nations of antiquity.
Several of these stone groups seem to have
been originally surrounded with a stone circle,
which circles have been almost always regarded as monuments to the dead. Ossian
frequently alludes to the custom of the ancient
inhabitants of the Highlands—the Celts—of
marking the resting-place of their departed
heroes. "Four grey stones mark the grave of
the hero," are lines often occurring with slight
variations in the poems of the Gaelic Homer.
These stones here at Abury immediately give
rise to the idea of their being monuments of
the dead—they look like grave-stones, especially at a distance. Perhaps here lie buried the
priests who formerly ministered in the ancient
temple of Abury. Here their successors may
have sacrificed to the soul of the deceased.

That the Druids believed in the doctrine of
immortality is supported by the witness of
ancient writers.   So did the race who inhabited Britain immediately after their religion
had been swept away—if there be any truth in
Ossian.   But when the Druids had gone, the
idea of an immortal soul became a very different conception—merely a shadowy being
seen in the mist rising in the vale or heard in
the wind of night.   The Druidical doctrine of
immortality was far more inspiring.   Here it is
in the lines of Lucan, a Roman poet:

> " The Druids now, while arms are heard no more,
>   Old mysteries and barbarous rites restore,
>   A tribe who singular religion love,
>   And haunt the shady coverts of the grove.
>   To these, and these of all mankind alone,
>   The gods are sure revealed, or sure unknown,
>   If dying mortal's doom they sing aright,
>   No ghosts descend to dwell in dreadful night;
>   No parting souls to grisly Pluto go,
>   Nor seek the dreary silent shades below;
>   But forth they fly immortal of their kind,
>   And other bodies in new worlds they find;
>   Thus life for ever runs its endless race,
>   And like a line death but divides the space,
>   A stop which can but for a moment last,
>   A point between the future and the past.

Thrice happy they beneath their northern skies,
Who that worst fear—the fear of death—despise.
Hence they no cares for this frail being feel,
But rush undaunted on the pointed steel ;
Provoke approaching fate, and bravely scorn
To spare that life which must so soon return."

Rowe's " Lucan."

The passage is quoted by Richard of Cirencester in his *Ancient State of Britain.* It has
been noted by travellers in Persia that there
are in that country somewhat similar remains
to these at Abury—large stones standing on
end in groups. In connection with this a
passage of Pliny is interesting : " But why
should I commemorate those things with re-
gard to a thing which has passed over sea, and
reached the bounds of nature ? Britain at this
day celebrates it with so many wonderful ceremonies that she seems to have taught it to the
Persians." As the stone avenue approaches
Abury the stones are found placed closer together, seemingly in two rows. In one or two
places a row of stones crosses the avenue.
There may be seen around numerous tumuli,
sometimes scarcely elevated two feet above the
earth, at other times visible for miles ; here

single and alone, yonder in groups of two or three; some on the downs, some in the vale. These may, perhaps, commemorate secular chieftains, if the stones be held to be in memory of priests. This plain of Abury seems to be one vast graveyard. The Celts had a custom, it is said, of spending a night on or near the tumuli raised over their ancestors, in order to receive communications from their departed spirits. Such things may have been practised here. Wiltshire was originally inhabited by a tribe of Britons called the Belgæ.

"All the Belgæ," writes Richard of Cirencester, "are Allobroges or foreigners, and derived their origin from the Celts. The latter, not many ages before the arrival of Cæsar, quitted their native country, Gaul, which was conquered by the Romans and Germans, and passed over to this island." But the Celts were not the original inhabitants of Wiltshire, since, in another passage, he states that in the year of the world 3,600, or four centuries before Christ, the Senones emigrated from Britain, and in 3,650 the "Belgæ entered this country, and the Celts occupied the region

deserted by the Senones," who had gone to
"invade Italy and attack Rome." Hence it is
a question whether these memorials were
erected by the Senones or the Celts. They
may, perhaps, be the result of the labours of
two different tribes: the stones being the
monuments of one age, and the earth mounds,
or tumuli, of another.

The village of Abury is completely surrounded by a deep fosse and steep embankment, the latter outermost, hence it could never
have been constructed for defence. It is nearly
circular, very deep, and would enable a vast
multitude of people standing upon the mound
to witness the rites and ceremonies performed
at the altars by the priests within the circle,
the ditch being the division between the un-
initiated and the initiated. It may be observed
that when the fosse was dug the earth was
not thrown up exactly at its outer edge but
somewhat back, thus leaving a portion of
ground between the fosse and embankment.
The fosse was probably destined to answer the
same purpose as the stones which Moses is
recorded to have placed around Mount Sinai
to keep the assembled multitude from the sacred

ground within. There are at present four
entrances through the embankment to the
village. They are formed by as many roads,
on each side of which stand at this day huge
stones set on edge, like pillars. Some of these
stones are diamond-shaped. Abury Church
stands immediately without the embankment.
Somewhere about the centre of the enclosed
ground there stand three huge stones of great
height, some of which might form the end wall
of a good sized house, of such height and
breadth are they. They stand close to some
cottages, the grey, weather-beaten memorial of
former ages, that has stood the storms of twenty
centuries, beside the whitewashed, thatched,
perishable erections of the present, or at most
the last, generation. To the south of them,
in a field nearer the embankment, stand four
or five others, perhaps not so high, but broader,
and of a squarer shape. These may be from
fifteen to eighteen feet high. One of them
seems to have a hollow beneath it, into which,
an old man informed us, he had crept, when
a boy, but found it not to extend above the
length of his body. He was nearly suffocated
having found it difficult to withdraw without

assistance from the small size of the aperture into which he had imprudently advanced. Immediately without the embankment, further south beside the Marlborough road, stand two stones of smaller dimensions, but still large, which seem disposed there to indicate the direction of Silbury Hill. Other stones are scattered about within the fosse, some so much sunk in the ground as to be hardly visible. There may not now, perhaps, be more than a score of stones remaining within the fosse, but these are of the largest size. Wonder has been expressed at the raising of such large stones to a perpendicular position. It merely required the command of unlimited labour. They were probably raised by heaping earth beneath them, by a combination of the inclined plane, wedge, and lever, in the same way as were the colossal statues of Egypt. The original form in which these stones were placed appears from a diagram, made some two hundred years since by Aubrey, to have been one large circle, inclosing two smaller ones ; the large circle of stones being set around immediately upon the inner edge of the fosse. The larger stones now remaining seem to have been the nucleus of the smaller circles, which were within the larger.

It is impossible to over estimate the solemn effect which this arrangement must have had when perfect, especially upon a rude and comparatively illiterate people. Even at this day, these venerable monuments of an age of which nothing is known with certainty, cannot be gazed upon without a sense of wonder almost amounting to awe. There they stand—the inscrutable sphinxes of England. What was the purpose for which they were erected? What have they witnessed? What is their meaning? Antiquarians seem to concur in assigning them an earlier date than Stonehenge since the stones at Salisbury bear the marks of tools—and these are unhewn—but they concur in nothing more. A Phœnician, a Celtic, a British, a Saxon, and even a Hindoo origin has been assigned them, the last by a writer in the *Philosophical Magazine* who produces many arguments in favour of his theory. He states that Britain was designated as the " White Island" in some sacred writings of the Hindoos. Britain is termed the White Island in several old Welsh documents. Richard of Cirencester states that Britain was first cultivated and inhabited one thousand years before Christ, "when it was visited by the Greek and Phœnician merchants." The Danes had a custom of performing great judicial ceremonies in stone circles, but they do not appear to have held this part of Britain long enough to warrant the assignment of Abury to them. It is mentioned by no ancient writer. A Roman road runs close by, but their historians say nothing of it. Abury is still a mystery.

A short distance from Abury is Silbury Hill,[1] another standing puzzle to antiquarians. It is a conical hill, very steep-sided, perhaps a hundred paces in circumference, and of great height,[2] having much the appearance of a barrow, and is evidently a work of man, since the places from whence the earth was taken can still be traced. It has been twice opened, once[3] by a shaft from the top, once by a horizontal opening[4]—but without leading to any discovery

---

[1] "The hugest tumulus, not only in Britain, but in Europe."—*Worth*.

[2] According to Dean Merewether, it is 125 feet high and 1,550 feet round, and covers nearly five acres.

[3] 1777.   [4] 1849.

that threw light upon the subject. A tradition, mentioned by Aubrey, states that it was raised as a monument over King Lil or Sil, who was buried on horseback, and this whilst a posset of milk was seething. The tradition may contain the germs of truth. It does not seem to have been connected with Abury, since it is not visible from there. The earth was probably carried up in baskets, and the enormous number of men employed in the work is intimated by that part of the legend which says it was thrown up in the short time that a posset of milk took in seething. King Charles II., in company with the Duke of York, once ascended this remarkable mound. The king commissioned Aubrey to prepare an account of Abury, which he accordingly did, and states therein that, in his opinion, the church and many of the houses may have been built of the stones which were found, the circles having been broken for that purpose. It may be mentioned in connection with the legend of King Sil that Herodotus mentions a custom of burial on horseback as prevalent amongst the Scythians, though not practised towards the persons of their kings. He also states that they threw up a heap of earth over the deceased.

Ancient coins, supposed to be British, are said to be frequently picked up by the ploughboys in the adjacent fields, especially after the heavy rains have washed away the soil. At a distance of perhaps two miles south of Abury there runs along the ridge of the downs a fosse and embankment, called Wansditch or dyke, more commonly the " Devil's Dyke." The country folk maintain that it runs through England. It was probably the boundary-line of an ancient kingdom. Upon the summit of a down at some distance can be seen a pillar. It was erected by the Marquis of Lansdowne. Here is Oldbury Castle another ancient encampment, and further on lies Heddington, a place which is a mine of wealth to an archæologist.

Abury is by some supposed to have been a temple erected by worshippers of the snake, by others as a temple of the sun. Both may be right, since snakes are remarkably fond of sunshine, and were the emblems of health, of which the sun was, and is, the great dispenser. Yet both may nevertheless be wrong, so impenetrable is the mist of antiquity which hangs over this mysterious monument of bygone times.

CHAPTER VIII

THE OXFORD ROAD

ONE mile below Kingshill Hill, Swindon, a footpath branches off from the road upon the right hand. It leads to Lydiard Tregoze. It is a strange and very ancient village. Modern improvements and modern innovations do not seem to have penetrated here, though red-bricked houses may be seen at Shaw, a short distance away. Here, deep in a combe, or valley, half hidden by trees, stand three or four old houses, whose stone tiling immediately renders evident their antiquity. The church is invisible until the pedestrian arrives before it, so numerous are the trees. It stands exactly in front of the seat of Lord Bolingbroke, much in the same way as did the old church at Swindon, though this is even nearer. Lydiard Park lies just

beyond. It was formerly famous for the rear-
ing of "young things," *i.e.* cattle.

Lydiard and the neighbourhood are remarkably well wooded. Oak is abundant, though
it is observed that the trees never reach that
enormous size which astonishes one in other
localities. There is a curious legend about
these oak trees. Ages ago a member of the
Bolingbroke family rendered some important
service to an English monarch. In return he
received a grant of the lands of Lydiard until
he should have taken three crops off them,
after which they were to revert to the Crown.
The wily nobleman had the lands sown with
acorns and hazel nuts, which shot up into oaks
and hazel woods, and the Bolingbrokes have
not cleared their first crop yet. Such is the
story. The Bolingbrokes have certainly been
connected with Lydiard Tregoze from time
immemorial. The name of Bolingbroke is very
celebrated, and frequently occurs in English
history. Shakespeare has immortalised it in
Richard II. It was then borne by a son of
John of Gaunt, who afterwards became king.
St. John is the family name. It was from the
Lord Bolingbroke of his day that the poet

Pope derived much of that philosophy which he has embodied in the Essay on Man. That poem opens with these lines :—

> "Awake, my St. John ! leave all meaner things
> To low ambition, and the pride of kings."

It is probable that the concluding lines in the fourth Epistle of that celebrated Essay were addressed to his friend St. John, Lord Bolingbroke :—

> "Come then, my friend, my genius, come along ;
> Oh master of the poet, and the song !
> And while the Muse now stoops, or now ascends,
> To man's low passions, or their glorious ends,
> Teach me, like thee, in various nature wise,
> To fall with dignity, with temper rise ;
> Form'd by thy converse, happily to steer
> From grave to gay, from lively to severe ;
> Correct with spirit, eloquent with ease,
> Intent to reason, or polite to please.
> Oh ! while along the stream of time thy name
> Expanded flies, and gathers all its fame ;
> Say, shall my little bark attendant sail,
> Pursue the triumph, and partake the gale?
> When statesmen, heroes, kings, in dust repose
> Whose sons shall blush their fathers were thy foes,
> Shall then this verse to future age pretend
> Thou wert my guide, philosopher, and friend?
> That, urged by thee, I turn'd the tuneful art
> From sounds to things, from fancy to the heart ;

> For wits' false mirror held up nature's light;
> Showed erring pride, whatever is, is right;
> That reason, passion, answer one great aim;
> That true self-love and social are the same;
> That virtue only makes our bliss below,
> And all our knowledge is, ourselves to know."

These lines finish the Essay, and contain the essence of that philosophy which he had before presented in a more expanded form. St. John, Viscount Bolingbroke, was a celebrated member of the ministry of Queen Anne. Pope was several times in North Wilts, and resided for a considerable period at Cirencester with his friend, Lord Bathurst. In Bathurst Park is still shown the poet's seat.

The game-preserves of Lydiard are now much noted, so that it is a common observation that in driving along the roads near by it is necessary to go slowly and whip the pheasants out of the way, as if they were a flock of sheep. As many as 800 head of game have been shot in a single battue.

Lydiard is a very ancient place. It is now known as Tregoze, but was formerly Lydiard Ewyas. Lydiard was an inhabited spot in the days of William the Conqueror, as appears from the following ancient lines copied from a genealogical tablet in the church, of which more presently. The verses are somewhat strangely distributed in the original, and there are divers opinions as to the proper manner of reading them ; but the following disposition seems most natural. The same tablet states that they are " Some ancient remains of Sir Richard St. George, Knight, Garter King-at-Arms, relating to ye pedigree of St. John, written in the year 1615, and transcribed in this present year, 1694 " :—

"When conquering William won by force of sword
  The famous island, now called Brittan's land,
  Of Lydiard then was Ewyas only Lord,
  Whose heir to Tregoz, linckt in marriage band :
  That Tregoz, a great Baron in his age,
  By her had issue the Lord Grauntson's wife ;
  Whose daughter Patshull took in marriage
  And Beauchamp theirs ; Beauchamp, with happy life,
  Was blessed with a daughter, whence did spring
  An heir to St. John who did Lydiard bring.
  Thus course of time, by God's almighty power,
  Hath kept this land of Lydiard in one race,
  Five hundred forty-nine years, and now more,
  Where at this day is St. John's dwelling-place ;
  Noe ! noe ! he dwells in heaven whose anchored faith
  Fixed on God accounted life but death."

" Five hundred and forty-nine years " have now (1867) increased to eight hundred and one—a long, long vista of years to look back upon.

There are numerous monuments to the Bolingbrokes, or rather the St. Johns, in Lydiard Church. The church is ancient, and contains several stained glass windows. The windows of the north aisle contain a small quantity of very old stained glass. Over the entrance door there is a carved figure of a woman, pinched and miserable, as if in the last agonies of starvation. The legend runs that it is in memory of a person who died from toothache. The chancel is supported upon pillars, and the roof presents the likeness of the sun, moon, and stars ; it is, in fact, a representation of the sky. The chancel forms a vast canopy over the monuments of the St. Johns, whose remains lie mouldering in the extensive vaults beneath.

A full-length gilt statue of a St. John, in the dress and with the flowing locks of the Cavaliers, stands against the south wall of the chancel. Two smaller figures are on either hand, drawing back a curtain which reveals the cavalier. Tradition tells a strange tale about this statue, which is said to represent a Royalist warrior, who had constructed for himself a dress, or armour, of brass, impervious save in one spot, and who passed safely through the dangers of the Civil War, until he was at length betrayed by his servant. In the chancel itself, somewhat to the south of the communion table, is a magnificent monument to John St. John, knight and baron, and his two wives, Anna and Margarita. It is dated A.D. 1634.

Beneath a canopy, itself ornamented with divers small figures, lies the effigy of the baron, apparently executed in alabaster, and at full length. He is in armour. Full-length figures of his two wives lie, one on either side, and on the breast of one lies an infant. All three are in an attitude of repose. The execution is excellent, and so marked are the features that it may be conjectured they are, to a certain extent, correct copies of the originals. Five sons kneel at the head of their parents, and three daughters at their feet.[1] It is, perhaps,

---

[1] " At their feet are a spread eagle and three figures of girls kneeling, and at their heads are five boys in the same attitudes. From the tomb rise eight Corinthian columns

the most magnificent monument in the neighbourhood.

Near by, on the north wall, at a considerable
elevation, is a monument to another St. John
and his lady, dated 1633.[1] The figures here

of black marble, supporting an arch and entablature, with
several figures and armorial bearings. On the entablature
is the following inscription :—

"D. S.

"Johannes St. John Miles et Baronettus, annum agens
XLIX um, mortalitatis suæ memor H. M. M. P. C. Anno
M.D.C.XXXIIII et sibi et Uxoribus suis Annæ sc. et Mar-
garettæ. Anna Filia fuit Th. Leyghton Eq. Auæ, ex Eliz.
Conjuge Gentis Knowleisæ, et Reginæ Elizabeth ætam
virtutis quam cognationis ergo in Deliciis. Vixit annos
XXXVII eximiis animi et corporis et gratiæ muneribus
datata, rarum virtutis et pietatis exemplum; XIII Liberorum
superstitium mater, tandem arumnosis ultimi puerperii
agonibus diu conflictata et demum victa, fugit in cœlum
XIII Cal. Octob. M.D.C.XXVIII. — Margaretta Filia
fuit Gul. Whitmor, Armig., de Apley, Provinciæ Salop.
Vivit LVIII um agens annum, virtutis laude spectabilis et
bonis operibus intenta; in istud hujus familiæ Requiet-
orium, suo tempore (ni aliter ipsa olim statuerit), aggre-
ganda."—(Britton's *Beauties of Wiltshire.*)

[1] M.S. Fœminarum optimæ Dominæ *Katherinæ Mompesson*,
forma, pudicitia constantia, pietate, omni virtutum genere,
præstantissimæ, Johannis St. John de Liddiard Tregose,
Baroneth Sororis natu maximæ, Egidii Mompesson ex
antiqua Familia de Bathampton in Comitatu Wiltis Equitis
Aurati Conjugis charissimæ, qui quidem Egidius viginti sex

are not full size. The knight is seated facing his lady, with an open book before him, which he appears to be silently regarding. His lady is also seated, in an attitude of melancholy reflection, with her left hand upon a skull, which 'rests upon her knee, and the other supporting her head. Monuments to later members of the St. John family adjoin these. In the body of the church, but against the south wall, is a canopied monument to Nicholas Seynt John [1]

annorum Matrimonii fœliciter peractus, minime oblitus (adhuc superstes) hoc Sepulchrum condidit, ubi suas etiam cineres (quum occiderit) reponi jussit. Obiit XXVIII. Mart. A.D. 1633.

[1] Jacent hic, Optime Lector, sub spe beatæ Resurrectionis, reposita corpora *Nicholai Seynt Jhon*, Armigeri, et Elizabethæ conjugis suæ, Regi Edoardo, Reginæ Mariæ, et Reginæ Elizabethæ è selectorum stipatorum numero, quos vulga pentionarios vocantur : fuit cumque apud Principem locum obtinens mortem obiit, Elizabetha ipsius Uxor filia fuit Richardi Blunt, Militis ; ex esque genuit tres filios et quinque filias ; Johannem, Oliverum, Richardum ; Elizabetham, Catherinam, Helinoram, Dorotheam, at que Janam. Johannes filius natu maximus in Uxorem duxit filiam Gualteri Hungerford, Militis ; Oliverus et Richardus vivunt adhuc cœlibes. Elizabetha filia natu maxima nupsit Seynt George, Comitatus Cantabrigiensis ; Catharina Webb ; Helinora Cave, Comitatus Northamptoniensis ; Dorothea Egiocke, Warvicensis ; Jana vero Nicholas, Comitatus Wiltesiensis. Ipse Nicholas Seynt John ex hac vita dis-

and his lady, dated 1522.   Beneath the canopy
kneel the figures of the knight and his lady,
but they are not full size.   He is in armour,
and has a sword girded to his side.   It may be
remarked that the spelling of the name here
"Seynt John" is a nearer approach to its ordinary pronunciation in the neighbourhood
than St. John.   Close to the monument there
is a brass plate affixed to the wall in memory
of George Richard St. John, dated 1824.

The genealogical tablet, which has been
already referred to, is affixed, together with
several others, to the south wall of the chancel,
within the rails around the communion table.
Above the tablets is a portrait of Queen Elizabeth, evidently intended to represent her in her
earlier days.   Over this stands a gilt imperial

---

cessit octavo die Novembris, Anno Domini 1589 ; Elizabetha vero ipsius Conjux ex hac vita discessit undecimo die
Augusti Anno Domini 1587 ; insignem reliquentes trop-
hæum posteris suis et famæ puræ et vitæ integræ.   Johannes
Seynt John illorum filius hoc illis de se optime meritis et
finis parentibus pietatis ergo Monumentum posuit.

Anno Domini 1592.

Nobis est Christus et in vita et in morte lucrum.   Tem-
pora qui longæ speras felicia vitæ, Spes tua te fallit, testes
utrique sumus.

eagle. The first tablet brings down the genea-
logy of the St. Johns from the days of William
the Conqueror, 1066 A.D., and from William
Rufus, 1083 A.D., to 1654. All these tablets
are covered with escutcheons and heraldic devices, the coats of arms of the persons referred
to, which devices would themselves fill a
volume, and exhibit every form of heraldic
imagery. Another shows their alliance,
affinity, and consanguinity to Henry VII. and
to Queen Elizabeth, beneath whose portrait are
the words " Thirty-two Ancestors." The third
tablet reveals the alliances which the St. Johns
have made with other noble families during the
course of so many centuries. The "ancient
remains of Sir Richard St. George," already
given, are inscribed at the foot of the centre
tablet. It is, no doubt from—

" That Tregoz, a great Baron in his age,"

that Lydiard takes its present name of Lydiard
Tregoze, in order to distinguish it from
Lydiard Millicent, another village near by.
All these tablets open, and reveal other genea-
logies beneath. The two centre ones when
thrown open reveal a life-like portrait of John

St. John, knight and baron, full length, with
his wife Lucy, daughter of Sir Walter Hungerford.[1]   Six children, of divers ages and heights,
cluster round upon the right hand.   This Lucy
married again after the death of St. John, and
the two figures upon the left hand are probably
herself and her second husband.   The date is
1594, though the same inscription states that
the tablet was not erected until 1615.   These
portraits are remarkably life-like, and have none
of that stiffness which usually gives family
paintings so disagreeable a harshness.   The
colours are still fresh and well preserved.   The
smiling, blue-eyed, brown-haired, hearty, En-
glish-looking John St. John seems almost
about to start forward from the wall.   The
description which Sir Walter Scott gives of

[1] " Here lieth the body of Sir John St. John, Knt., who
married Lucy, daughter and coheire of Sir Walter Hungerford, of Farley, Knt., by whom he had issue Walter, that
died young, Sir John St. John, Knt. and Baronet, Oliver,
that died young, Katherine, Anne, Jane, Elinor, Barbara,
Lucy, and Martha, that died a child.   He deceased 20th
September, 1594.   She was secondly married to Sir Anthony
Hungerford, Knt., by whom she had Edward, Briget, and
Jane, and then died the 4th June, 1598.   This was erected
by Sir John St. John, Knt. and Baronet, in the year 1655,
the 20th of July."

King Richard Cœur-de-Lion might have been
taken from this portrait of St. John, so singular
is the coincidence. There is the same fearless,
open, frank look which is said to have charac-
terized the English hero of the Crusades.

On the floor of the chancel is a very ancient
stone slab to one Kiblewhite, the figures much
worn with feet. Several helmets are suspended in divers parts of the church. The
effect of these numerous monuments to departed greatness is very solemn, and is
increased by the dim light from the stained
glass windows. Here sleep the warrior and
the statesman, men celebrated in their day,
their names in all men's mouths, now only
known by the epitaph and escutcheon. Who
remembers the great baron Tregoz? Who
thinks of him when he hears of Lydiard Tregoze? Ewgas is still less remembered. The
St. John commemorated by Pope runs the
best chance of immortality. Those who fought
with doublehanded swords, with battle-axe and
lance, have long been forgotten; it is only the
Muse who confers immortality. Ink is more
durable than iron. Yonder hang the heavy
helmets of a forgotten generation. Who re-

member the wearers? None but the genea-
logist, and he only after much cogitation.
Eight hundred years is a long time to look
back upon. What innumerable events must
have been witnessed by those who bore the
name, or were the ancestors of the St. Johns in
that long course of centuries? They seem to
have shared in the bounty of William the Conqueror; they no doubt fought in the French
wars, in the Wars of the Red and White
Roses; they were not backward in the times of
the Great Rebellion. They have escaped all
dangers, and survive yet. For those who
sleep beneath the cold stone pavement of this
ancient church the lines might make a good
epitaph :—

> " The knights are dust,
>   Their good swords are rust,
>   Their souls are with the saints, we trust ! "

Lydiard is now rarely the residence of the
present Lord Bolingbroke. Lydiard Millicent
is a pleasant village. Purton lies immediately
beyond it. It is a large place, and dates from
very ancient days. In Domesday Book[1] the

---

[1] " The same church (S. Mary at Malmesbury) holds
Piritone."—*Domesday* reference.

name is spelt Piritone. It is considered to
mean Pear-tree town. A considerable part of
Purton then belonged to the Abbey of Malmesbury. Purton Church is a peculiar structure,
somewhat resembling Wanborough, there being
both a tower and a spire. There are several
large niches outside the tower, which probably
once contained images, which have now disappeared. Purton was once the residence of
Edward Hyde, who afterwards became the
celebrated Earl of Clarendon, Lord Chancellor
in the time of King Charles II. His *History of the Great Rebellion* is the basis of all
other histories of that great period. He was
peculiarly qualified from his attendance upon
the king, and from the ready access which he
had to State documents, to perform such a task.
It is an enormous work, judged by the modern
standard, and extends to over two thousand
closely printed pages. Whilst residing at Purton, in the character of a private person, he was
chosen a member of Parliament both by the
adjacent town of Wootton Bassett, and a more
distant place, but preferred " serving his neigh-
bours" of the former place. The house in
which he lived is, or was lately, the property of

the Earl of Shaftesbury. Purton has been in some sense connected with another distinguished man. The celebrated Lord Clive married Margaret Maskelyne, daughter of Edmund Maskelyne, of Purton. Anthony Goddard was of Purton, in 1737.

Purton was formerly famous for its morrice-dancing,[1] an old English pastime which has almost died out. The old custom of mumming[2] at Christmas seems also rapidly going out of date, though it is still kept up in the outlying country districts. Hand-bell ringing will probably follow, and then there will be little left indeed that savours of the pastimes of old England. Many lament the change, which is charged upon the railroads and canals.

There is a splendid view from the summit of Pevenhill, Purton. It is said that no less than twenty-six church towers, or spires, can be counted on a clear day. Birdlip Hill, in Gloucestershire, is then visible. Immediately

---

[1] Douce's *Illustrations of Shakespeare*, published in 1839, has some good notes on morris-dancing.

[2] There is an excellent chapter on the Wiltshire Mummers in Mr. Morris's *Swindon Fifty Years Ago*.

beneath lie Braden Woods. Braden Forest was anciently of great extent, and was part of the property of the Duke of Lancaster. Monarchs hunted the deer in the depths of Braden Forest. King Henry the Eighth " rode a-hunting " there. It is still a large wood.

The village of Fasterne lies at no very great distance from Purton. Here, says tradition, was born King Richard, or else a Duke of York, probably the latter.

Cleeve Pipard is a village lying between Broad Hinton and Purton. It is an ancient place. The pronunciation is Cliff. The manor of Cleeve Pipard was, in the year 1530, on the thirteenth of April, transferred from William Dauntsey, Alderman of London, to John Goddard, gent, of Aldborne. John Goddard, Esq., was the ancestor of the present owner of the estate, H. N. Goddard, Esq. The old Swindon family of the Bradfords is connected by marriage with the Goddards of Cleeve Pipard.

Most of these places—Lydiard Tregoze, Lydiard Millicent, Purton, Cleeve Pipard— were visited by Aubrey, when he passed through North Wilts, about two centuries since.

Fairford lies at a considerable distance from Swindon, and in another county, but is of a celebrity so great that it can scarcely be passed over in silence.

The church is the cause of its fame. It is a fine old structure, built more than three centuries ago by a person of the name of John Tame, in the year 1493. John Tame was a merchant and seafaring man, and chanced to take a prize ship destined for Rome. The prize was highly valuable on account of a quantity of magnificent stained glass which was found on board, and so greatly delighted was Tame with his capture that, bringing it to England, he built a church to put it in. The church was then dedicated to the Virgin Mary, and the stained glass has remained ever since, the wonder and admiration of all who have seen it. The design is said to have been that of Albrecht Dürer, the celebrated artist,[1] but doubt has been thrown upon this by the

---

[1] Jefferies described Dürer as an Italian artist, but he was German by birth, and did not go to Italy till 1505.

WEST WINDOW, FAIRFORD CHURCH.

fact that at the date when this glass was made
he had not yet reached his twentieth year,
while it is well known that a length of time
is necessary to complete such work. These
windows number no less than twenty-eight,
and the paintings are from scenes in the Bible.

The choir windows contain the various
events that attended the crucifixion of Christ ;
these windows, together with some upon the
western side of the church, are somewhat
larger than the others. Other windows portray
the apostles, prophets, martyrs, fathers, con-
fessors, and persecutors of the church, in short
a sort of ecclesiastical history. These figures
are full size. Hell and damnation are represented at the west end with such horrible
minuteness of detail that we understand this
window is usually kept covered. The paintings
are well preserved and the colours fresh, while
so excellent is the execution that Sir Anthony
Vandyke was of opinion that they could not
be surpassed by the pencil. It is scarcely
probable that Dürer could have designed these
extensive windows ere he had attained his
twentieth year ; or, if he had designed them,
that they could have been executed in so short

a time as must necessarily have elapsed from
the date of the design to the capture of the
ship by John Tame. In all probability the
fame of Dürer has usurped that of another
less celebrated. During the Civil Wars, when
such articles ran a great risk of destruction at
the hands of the Parliamentarians, these paintings were turned wrong side uppermost, and
so escaped being smashed. Bishop Corbett,
who died on January 28th, 1635, and was,
says one contemporary, "the best poet of all
the bishops of that age," seems to have visited
Fairford, since the following two poems are
supposed to have been written by him upon
Fairford windows :—

> "Tell me, you anti-saints, why brass
> With you is shorter lived than glass ?
> And why the saints have scap't their falls
> Better from windows than from walls ?
> Is it because the Brethren's fires
> Maintain a glass-house at Blackfryars ?
> Next which the church stands north and south,
> And east and west the preacher's mouth,
> Or is't because such painted ware
> Resembles something that you are,
> Soe pyde, so seeming, soe unsound,
> In manners and in doctrine found.

That out of emblematick witt
You spare yourselves in sparing it ?
If it be soe, then, Fairford boast
Thy Church hath kept what all have lost ;
And is preserved from the bane
Of either war, or Puritane :
Whose life is coloured in thy paint
The inside dross, the outside saint."

"UPON FAIREFORD WINDOWES."

" I knowe no painte of poetry
Can mend such colore'd imagry
In sullen inke, yet (Fayreford) I
May relish thy fair memory.
Such is the echoes fainter sound,
Such is the light when the sunn's drown'd,
So did the fancy look upon
The work before it was begun.
Yet when those showes are out of sight,
My weaker colors may delight.
Those images doe faith fullie
Report true feature to the eie,
As you may think each picture was
Some visage in a looking-glass ;
Not a glass window face, unless
Such as Cheapside hath, where a press
Of painting gallants, looking out,
Bedeck the casement rounde about.
But these have holy phisnomy ;
Each paine instructs the laity
With silent eloquence ; for heere
Devotions leads the eie, not eare.

To not the cathechisinge paint,
Whose easie phrase doth soe acquainte
Our sense with Gospell, that the Creede
In such a hand the weake may reade,
Such tipes e'er yett of vertue bee,
And Christ as in a glass we see—
When with a fishinge rod the clarke
St. Peter's draught of fish doth marke.
Such is the scale, the eye, the finn,
You'd thinke they strive and leap within;
But if the nett, which holdes them, brake
Hee with his angle some would take.
But would you walke a turn in Paules,
Looke up, one little pane inrouls
A fairer temple. Flinge a stone,
The church is out at the windowe flowne.
Consider not, but aske your eies,
And ghosts at midday seem to rise;
The saintes there seemeing to descend,
Are past the glass and downwards bend.
Look there ! The Devill ! all would cry,
Did they not see that Christ was by.
See where he suffers for thee !   See
His body taken from the tree !
Had ever death such life before?
The limber corps, be-sully'd o'er
With meagre paleness, does display
A middle state 'twixt flesh and clay.
His arms and leggs, His head and crown,
Like a true lamb-kin dangle downe;
Whoe can forbeare, the grave being nigh,
To bringe fresh ointment in His eye?
The wondrous art hath equal fate,

Unfixt, and yet, inviolate.
The Puritans were sure deceav'd
Whoe thought those shaddowers mov'd and heav'd
So held from stonnige Christ; the winde
And boysterous tempests were so kinde
As on His image not to prey
Whome both the winde and seas obey.
At Momus bee not amaz'd;
For if each Christian's heart were glaz'd
With such a windowe, then each brest
Might be his owne evangelist."

INDEX

www.ingramcontent.com/pod-product-compliance
Lightning Source LLC
Chambersburg PA
CBHW020856270326
41928CB00006B/733